HOW TO
RELAX

THICH NHAT HANH

PARALLAX
PRESS

BERKELEY, CALIFORNIA

Parallax Press
P.O. Box 7355
Berkeley, California 94707
parallax.org

Parallax Press is the publishing division of
Plum Village Community of Engaged Buddhism, Inc.
Printed by Friesens, Altona, MB, Canada, employee owned
and operated

Cover and text design by Debbie Berne
Edited by Rachel Neumann
Illustrations by Jason DeAntonis

ISBN: 978-1-941529-08-9

Library of Congress Cataloging-in-Publication Data
is available upon request.

8 9 / 22

CONTENTS

NOTES
ON RELAXING

You don't need to set aside special time for resting and relaxing. You don't need a special pillow or any fancy equipment. You don't need a whole hour. In fact, now is a very good time to relax.

You are probably breathing in and out right this moment. If you can close your eyes for a moment, do so. This will help you pay attention to your breath. Your body is doing so many things right now. Your heart is beating. Your lungs are inhaling and exhaling air. Blood is traveling through your veins. Without effort, your body is both working and relaxed.

RESTING

Whenever animals in the forest are wounded, they rest. They look for a very quiet place and just stay there without moving for many days. They know it's the best way for their body to heal. During this time they may not even eat or drink. The wisdom of stopping and healing is still alive in animals, but we human beings have lost the capacity to rest.

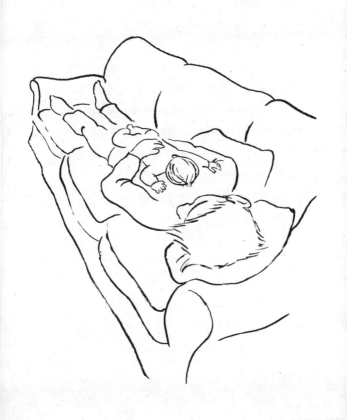

HEALING

We human beings have lost confidence in the body just knowing what to do. If we have time alone with ourselves, we panic and try to do many different things. Mindful breathing helps us to relearn the art of resting. Mindful breathing is like a loving parent cradling a baby, saying, "Don't worry, I'll take good care of you; just rest."

AWARENESS OF BREATHING

Your breathing is a stable, solid ground where you can take refuge. No matter what thoughts, emotions, and perceptions are going on inside you, your breath is always there, like a faithful friend. Whenever you're carried away by thinking, overwhelmed by strong emotions, or feeling restless and dispersed, return to your breathing. Bring body and mind together and anchor your mind. Become aware of the air coming in and going out of your body. With awareness of the breath, our breathing naturally becomes light, calm, and peaceful. At any time of the day or night, whether you're walking, driving, working in the garden, or sitting at the computer, you can return to the peaceful refuge of your own breath.

RESTING POEM

At any moment, we can say this small poem to ourselves and take a mini-rest. This poem is like a tiny vacation, except that it brings you back to your true home instead of taking you away from it.

Breathing in, I know I am breathing in.
Breathing out, I know I am breathing.out.

You can even shorten this poem; it works just as well:

In.
Out.

FOLLOWING THE BREATH

To increase your mindfulness and concentration, gently and easily follow your in-breath and out-breath all the way through. Just sitting and following your breathing can bring a lot of joy and healing.

Breathing in, I follow my in-breath all the way through.
Breathing out, I follow my out-breath all the way through.

CALM WATER

Each of us is like the waves and also like the water. Sometimes we're excited, noisy, and agitated like the waves. Sometimes we're tranquil like still water. When water is calm, it reflects the blue sky, the clouds, and the trees. Sometimes, whether we're at home, work, or school, we become tired, agitated, or unhappy and we need to transform into calm water. We already have calmness in us; we just need to know how to make it manifest.

MEDITATION

To meditate means to pay full attention to something. It doesn't mean to run away from life. Instead it's an opportunity to look deeply into ourselves and into the situation we're in.

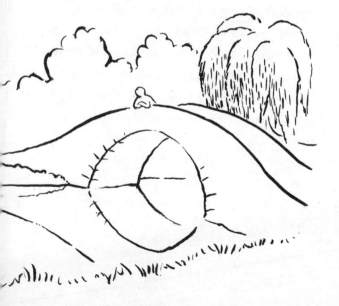

STOPPING: THE FIRST ASPECT OF MEDITATION

Meditation has two aspects. The first is stopping (*shamatha* in Sanskrit). We run throughout our whole life, chasing after some idea of happiness. Stopping means to stop our running, our forgetfulness, and our being caught in the past or the future. We come home to the present moment where life is available. The present moment contains every moment. Here we can touch our ancestors, our children, and their children, even if they haven't been born yet. We calm our body and emotions through the practice of mindful breathing, mindful walking, and mindful sitting. Shamatha is also the practice of concentrating, so we can live deeply each moment of our life and touch the deepest level of our being.

STOP FIRST

If we can't rest, it's because we haven't stopped running. We began running a long time ago. We continue to run, even in our sleep. We think that happiness and well-being aren't possible in the present. If you can stop and establish yourself in the here and the now, you will see that there are many elements of happiness available in this moment, more than enough for you to be happy. Even if there are a few things in the present that you dislike, there are still plenty of positive conditions for your happiness. When you walk in the garden, you may see that a tree is dying and so you feel sad and aren't able to enjoy the rest of the garden that is still beautiful. If you look again, you can see that the garden is still beautiful, and you can enjoy it.

LOOKING DEEPLY: THE SECOND ASPECT OF MEDITATION

The second aspect of meditation is looking deeply (*vipashyana* in Sanskrit) in order to see the true nature of things. Understanding is a great gift. Your daily life conducted in mindfulness is also a great gift; this too is the practice of meditation. Mindfulness carries within it concentration and understanding.

MINDFULNESS IN DAILY LIFE

Mindfulness is the continuous practice of touching deeply every moment of daily life. To be mindful is to be truly present with your body and your mind, to harmonize your intentions and actions, and to be in harmony with those around you. We don't need to make a separate time for this outside of our daily activities. We can practice mindfulness in every moment of the day—in the kitchen, the bathroom, or the garden, and as we go from one place to another. We can do the same things we always do—walking, sitting, working, eating, and so on—with mindful awareness of what we're doing. Our mind is with our actions.

A RELAXED POSITION

What is your most relaxed position?
Sometimes we think we can only relax if we
are lying down. But we can also sit in a relaxed
position. Your posture can be upright and not
rigid. Relax your shoulders. See if it's possible
to sit with no tension in your body.

HEALING ENERGY

If you can sit in meditation on your own, quietly and peacefully, that is already relaxing and healing. Even if nobody else knows you are meditating, the energy you produce is very beneficial for you and for the world. But if you sit with others, if you walk and work with others, the energy is amplified, and you will create a powerful collective energy of mindfulness for your own healing and the healing of the world. It's something one person cannot do alone. Don't deprive the world·of this essential spiritual food.

COLLECTIVE ENERGY
OF HEALING

Usually we think of relaxing and healing as
things that happen when we are alone. But
many thousands of people have participated
in collective walking meditation and mass
sitting meditation in some of the world's busiest cities. People have walked mindfully and
peacefully around the Hoan Kiem Lake in
Hanoi. They have left footprints of peace and
freedom on the ancient streets and piazzas
of Rome. Thousands of us have sat in silence
and stillness in London's busy Trafalgar Square
and in Zucotti Park in New York City. Everyone
who participates and everyone who witnesses
this collective practice has a chance to get in
touch with the energy of peace, freedom, healing, and joy. The collective energy generated

on such occasions is a gift that we can offer

ourselves, one another, the city, and the world.

CULTIVATING JOY

We may think of joy as something that
happens spontaneously. But joy needs to
be cultivated and practiced in order to grow.
When we sit in mindfulness with others, it's
easier to sit. When we relax with others, it's
easier to relax. The collective energy can
help us when we're tired or when our mind
wanders. The collective energy can bring us
back to ourselves. This is why it's so important
to practice with others. At first we may worry
that we aren't doing sitting or walking meditation properly, and we may hesitate to practice
with others for fear of being judged. But we
all know how to sit and how to breathe. That's
all we have to do. After only a few moments
of concentrating on our breathing, we can
bring peace and calm to our body and mind.

We only need to pay attention to our in-breath and out-breath. Just focus on that. That's all it takes to begin to calm the agitation in your mind and body and restore stability and peace within yourself. The concentration of those around you will also support you as you begin to practice. Do this a little bit each day, alone or with others. When you train like this, it becomes easier and easier to return to your mindful breathing. The more you train yourself, the more easily you touch the depths of your consciousness, and the more easily you can generate the energy of compassion. Each one of us can do this.

PRACTICING JOY TOGETHER

We can't try hard to relax, just as we can't use
a lot of strict effort to be mindful. When we
practice together as a community, our practice
of mindfulness becomes more joyful, more
relaxed, and steady. We are bells of mindfulness for each other, supporting and reminding
each other along the path of practice. With the
support of the community, we can cultivate
peace and joy in ourselves, which we can
then offer to those around us. We cultivate
our solidity and freedom, our understanding and compassion. We practice looking
deeply to gain the sort of insight that can free
us from suffering, fear, discrimination, and
misunderstanding.

MINDFULNESS OF THE BODY

In our body there may be tension and pain. If we suppress or ignore this, then every day the tension and pain will grow and prevent us from experiencing the happiness that we should be able to experience. When we have tension in our body, we can't sleep well or eat well. Mindfulness of breathing can help us relax and bring peace to our body. We take care of our body first. We can take care of our mind later.

COMMUNICATING WITH OURSELVES

Sometimes we want to relax because we want to not think. That's wonderful; we all need non-thinking time. But that doesn't mean we should stop listening. When we stop thinking, we can start communicating with ourselves by listening to our bodies and our emotions. With all the technology we have, we need only a few seconds to get in contact with people who live very far away. But true communication with others can't happen unless we stop, relax, and listen to ourselves.

RESTORING WELLNESS

Releasing any tension and bringing calm to your body is the first step in restoring wellness. You can't heal your body if you don't pay attention to it. Bringing your mind home to your body, you become established in the here and the now. You have a chance to be aware, without judgment, of any pain, tension, or suffering in your body. This is the beginning of healing.

PEACEFUL BREATHING

When we begin practicing awareness of our breath, the breathing may not be very peaceful. It may be rushed, uneven, or shallow. This is because of the tensions in our body and the sadness and other preoccupations in our mind. Therefore, our breathing isn't peaceful. Breathing in and out, we concentrate just on our breathing. If we continue to practice awareness of breathing, our breathing becomes gentle, deeper, more peaceful, and the state of dispersion in our mind ceases. Here are three exercises to bring peace to the breath. The first is to recognize the in-breath as an in-breath, and the out-breath as an out-breath. The second is to recognize the length of the in-breath and out-breath. The third is to focus on the breath all the way through. This is concentration. We just observe the breath; we never force it. We allow it to be natural. With awareness of breathing, our breath naturally becomes deeper, slower, and more peaceful.

Breathing in, I know I'm breathing in.
Breathing out, I know I'm breathing out.

Breathing in, I see my breath is long or short.
Breathing out, I see my breath is long or short.

Breathing in, I follow my in-breath
all the way through.
Breathing out, I follow my out-breath
all the way through.

THE SOUND OF THE BELL

I started inviting the bell when I was sixteen years old, the age when I became a novice monk. We say, "invite the bell" rather than "strike the bell" because we think of the bell as a friend. We want to invite its sound into our bodies. Inviting a bell to sound is one very simple way to relax. When we hear the bell, we breathe in and we breathe out, and we take in that beautiful sound. That's it. If we don't have a bell, we can use another sound—a phone ringing, an airplane passing overhead, the chime of a clock, a timer on the computer, or the natural sounds around us. We can even use the sound of a jackhammer or a leaf blower.

BREATHING ROOM

Do you have a space dedicated to relaxing in your home? This doesn't have to be a big space. It could be a small corner (not your bed!) or anywhere in a room that is dedicated just to breathing and relaxing. This is not a space for eating or doing homework, or folding laundry or building anything. This is as essential as a place to eat, sleep, and go to the bathroom. We need a small space where we can take care of our nervous system and restore our tranquility and peace.

BRINGING PEACE TO
OUR TERRITORY

Each of us has a physical body, as well as feelings, perceptions, thoughts, emotions, and
a deep consciousness. These comprise our
territory; and each of us is a monarch ruling
over our territory. But we're not responsible
monarchs. There's disharmony and conflict
in our territory. We don't have the capacity to
restore peace and harmony. Instead of survey-
ing our territory, we escape and take refuge
in some form of consumption. Mindfulness is a
practice to give you the courage and energy
to go back and embrace your body and your
feelings and emotions, even if they're unpleasant. Even if it seems they may destroy you,
go back and embrace them and help them to
transform. If you're still afraid, ask friends in

the practice for support. Practicing walking meditation, conscious breathing, and eating meals in mindfulness, you cultivate the energy of mindfulness and you're able to reign peacefully over your territory.

LAZY DAY

Most of us have very scheduled lives and very full calendars. But do we have enough lazy days in our calendar? A lazy day is a day for us to be without any scheduled activities. We just let the day unfold naturally, timelessly. On this day we have a chance to reestablish the balance in ourselves. We may do walking meditation on our own or with a friend, or do sitting meditation in the forest. We might like to read a little or write home to our family or to a friend. It can be a day for us to look more deeply at our practice and at our relations with others. Or we may recognize that we simply need to rest. When we have unscheduled time, we tend to get bored, seek entertainment, or cast about for something to do. A lazy day is a chance to train ourselves not to

be afraid of doing nothing. You might think
that not doing anything is a waste of time. But
that's not true. Your time is first of all for you to
be—to be alive, to be peace.

BEING PEACE

The world needs joyous and loving people who are capable of just being. If you know the art of being peace, then you have the basis for your every action. The ground for action is to be, and the quality of being determines the quality of doing. Action must be based on non-action. People sometimes say, "Don't just sit there, do something." But we have to reverse that statement to say, "Don't just do something, sit there," in order to be in such a way that peace, understanding, and compassion are possible.

RELAXATION NEEDS INSIGHT

We know that there are those who try very
hard to be mindful, and yet they cannot relax.
They try to breathe and they try to walk; they
try very hard, and yet they're unable to
relax—because trying is not mindfulness.
It's not because you have the intention to
relax that you can relax. It's not because you
have the intention to stop that you can stop.
Mindfulness, true mindfulness, must carry
within it true view, insight. You need insight in
order to relax.

MINDFULNESS OF SOMETHING

Mindfulness is always mindfulness *of* something. We can be mindful of our breath, our footsteps, our thoughts, and our actions. Mindfulness requires that we bring all our attention to whatever we're doing, whether we're walking, breathing, brushing our teeth, or eating a snack. To be mindful is already to be awakened. If we can say with awareness, "Breathing in, I know I have a body," that is already insight. Because if we know we have a body, we can know how to take care of our body. If we want to reduce stress and tension, we need to be aware that we've been running a lot. True happiness isn't found in success, money, fame, or power. True happiness should be found in the here and the now. With that kind of insight you can truly relax.

RELAXING IN NATURE

When you walk in the hills, in a park, or along a riverbank, you can follow your breathing. When you feel tired or irritated, you can lie down with your arms at your sides, allowing all your muscles to relax, maintaining awareness of just your breath and your smile. Relaxing in this way is wonderful, and quite refreshing. You'll benefit a lot if you practice this several times a day. Your mindful breath and your smile will bring happiness to you and to those around you. There's nothing you could buy your loved ones that could give them as much true happiness as your gift of awareness, breathing, and smiling—and these precious gifts cost nothing.

HEALING OURSELVES,
HEALING THE EARTH

Mindfulness and a deep awareness of the
Earth can help us to handle pain and difficult
feelings. It can help us heal our own suffering and increase our capacity to be aware of
the suffering of others. With awareness of the
Earth's generosity, we can generate a pleasant
feeling. Knowing how to create moments of
joy and happiness is crucial for our healing. It's
important to be able to see the wonders of life
around us and to recognize all the conditions
for happiness that already exist. Then, with
the energy of mindfulness, we can recognize
and embrace our feelings of anger, fear, and
despair and transform them. We don't need
to become overwhelmed by these unpleasant emotions.

WAKING UP TO THE MOMENT

Walking meditation is a way of waking up to the wonderful moment we are living in. If our mind is caught, preoccupied with our worries and our suffering, or if we distract ourselves with other things while walking, we can't practice mindfulness; we can't enjoy the present moment. We're missing out on life. But if we're awake, then we'll see this is a wonderful moment that life has given us, the only moment in which life is available. We can value each step we take, and each step can bring us happiness because we're in touch with life, with the source of happiness, and with our beloved planet.

TRANSFORMING AN
UNPLEASANT SOUND

One day during a retreat in the mountains of
northern California there was a wildfire nearby.
All day long, during sitting meditation, walking meditation, and silent meals we heard the
sound of helicopters. In Vietnam during the
war, the sound of helicopters meant guns,
bombs, and death. At the retreat there were
many practitioners of Vietnamese origin who
had gone through the war, so the sound was
not pleasant for them, nor was it pleasant
for the other practitioners. But there was no
choice. So we chose to practice listening to
the sound of the helicopters with mindfulness.
With mindfulness, we could tell ourselves that
this is not a helicopter operating in a situation of war, but a helicopter that is helping to

extinguish the flames. With mindfulness, we transform our unpleasant feeling into a pleasant feeling of gratefulness. So we practiced breathing in and out with the sound of helicopters. And we survived very well. We made the sound of helicopters into something helpful. And we practiced:

I listen, I listen.
This sound of helicopters
brings me back
to the present moment.

SLEEPING

When you're in bed and unable to sleep, the best thing to do is to go back to your breathing. Resting is almost as beneficial as sleeping, and you'll know you're doing the best that you can. Bring peace to your breathing and your body so you can rest.

LEARNING TO REST

We have to relearn the art of resting. Even when we have a vacation, we don't know how to make use of it. Very often we are more tired after a vacation than before it. We should learn the art of relaxation and resting, and make some time each day to practice deep relaxation on our own or with others.

LEANING ON SNORING

Sometimes you have to share a room with someone who snores. You may get irritated. But with mindfulness you can bring about compassion. You can lean on the sound of snoring in order to go to sleep. Listen and say that this brings you home to the here and now. Then you can accept the snoring much more easily, and you can go to sleep thanks to the sound of snoring.

OUR IDEA OF HAPPINESS

Say you have a notion of happiness, an idea
about what will make you happy. That idea
has its roots in you and in your environment.
Your idea tells you what conditions you need
in order to be happy. You've entertained this
idea for ten or twenty years, and now you
realize that your idea of happiness is making
you suffer. Your idea may contain an element
of delusion, anger, or craving. These elements
are the substance of suffering. On the other
hand, you know that you have other kinds of
experiences: moments of joy, release, or true
love. You can recognize these as moments of
real happiness. When you've had a moment
of real happiness, it becomes easier to release
the objects of your craving, because you're

developing the insight that these objects will not make you happy.

Many people have the desire to let go, but they're not able to do so because they don't yet have enough insight; they haven't seen other alternatives, other doorways to peace and happiness. Fear is an element that prevents us from letting go. We're fearful that if we let go we'll have nothing else to cling to. Letting go is a practice; it's an art. One day, when you're strong enough and determined enough, you'll let go of the afflictions that make you suffer.

LETTING GO

To "let go" means to let go of *something*. That something may be an object of our mind, something we've created, like an idea, feeling, desire, or belief. Getting stuck on that idea could bring a lot of unhappiness and anxiety. We'd like to let it go, but how? It's not enough just to want to let it go; we have to recognize it first as being something real. We have to look deeply into its nature and where it has come from, because ideas are born from feelings, emotions, and past experiences, from things we've seen and heard. With the energy of mindfulness and concentration we can look deeply and discover the roots of the idea, feeling, emotion, or desire. Mindfulness and concentration bring about insight, and insight can help us release the object in our mind.

SOLITUDE

Being in solitude can help us relax. Solitude doesn't mean being by ourselves or away from civilization. Real solitude means we're not carried away by the crowd, by sorrows about the past, by worries about the future, or by strong emotions in the present. We don't lose our stability and our peace. We take refuge in our mindful breathing and come back to the present moment, and to the island of peace within ourselves. We enjoy our time with others, but we don't get lost in our interactions. Even in a busy marketplace, we can smile and breathe in peace, dwelling in the island of ourselves.

LETTING GO OF WORRYING

Our practice is to learn to take care of the present moment. Don't allow yourself to be lost in the past or the future. Taking good care of the present moment, we may be able to change the negative things from the past and prepare for a good future. We tend to worry about what will happen in the future. The practice helps us to come home to the present moment, to our body, our feelings, to the environment around us. When we breathe in and breathe out mindfully, our mind is brought back to our body, and we are truly there in order to take care of the present moment. If there's some stress, some tension in our body, we practice mindful breathing in order to release the tension, and that brings us relief. If

there's a painful feeling in us, we use mindfulness to embrace our feeling so that we can
get relief. The key point is that you are fully
there in the present moment, in the here and
now, to take care of yourself and what's happening around you. You don't think too much
about the future or project too much about
how it might be; and you're not trapped too
much in the past. You have to train yourself, to
learn how to go home to the present moment,
to the here and now, and to take care of that
moment, to take care of your body and your
feelings in this moment. As you learn how to
be in the present moment, you'll gain faith and
trust in your ability to handle the situation. You
learn how to take care of your feelings and
what's happening around you. That makes
you confident; and as your confidence grows,
you're no longer the victim of your worries.

HAPPINESS IS A
COLLECTIVE MATTER

We can learn to handle our own fear and
pain. After that, we can help other people,
because we have direct experience with how
to handle the fear and the pain. Suffering and
fear are not things that we just experience by
ourselves. Our fear and suffering is also the
suffering of our parents, our friends, and our
society. You are me and I am you. If something
wonderful happens to one of us, it happens to
all of us. If something awful happens to one of
us, it happens to all of us. This answer comes
from the insight of no-self. With the insight of
no-self you see that your suffering, your fear,
is a collective suffering. With the insight of
no-self, you see that happiness is a collective
happiness. We are not separated.

WALKING YOUR TALK

If you practice mindfulness to release the tension, stress, and pain in your body, you begin to feel better. Then, when you see a person who is tense, who has pain in his or her body, you can show him or her how to practice. That person will believe you because you have direct experience. You've walked your talk. That's why it's very important that we're able to do it for ourselves first. Just the way you live your life, the way you react to situations, can already be very helpful. Other people see you react in a peaceful and kind way, and they already begin to learn from you.

EFFORTLESSNESS

Do we need to make a special effort to see the beauty of the blue sky? Do we have to practice to be able to enjoy it? No, we just enjoy it. Each second, each minute of our lives can be like this. Wherever we are, at any time, we have the capacity to enjoy the sunshine, the presence of each other, even the sensation of our breathing. We don't need to go to China to enjoy the blue sky. We don't have to travel into the future to enjoy our breathing. We can be in touch with these things right now. It would be a pity if we were only aware of suffering.

LETTING GO OF STRESS

Stress accumulates in our body. The way
we eat, drink, and live takes its toll on our
well-being. Lying down and bringing gentle
awareness to our breath, we can realize rest
and recovery for our physical body. Find
space in your day when you can practice
mindful breathing and letting go of tensions.
In just five, ten, or twenty minutes, you can
reestablish mindfulness and dissipate stress.
When you have trouble sleeping, follow your
breathing in and breathing out. Bring your
awareness to the different parts of your body
in turn, and allow them to relax. Sometimes this
can help you get to sleep. The practice is still
very good even if you don't sleep, because it
nourishes you and allows you to rest.

LIFE IS DREADFUL
AND WONDERFUL

Meditation means being aware of what is going on—in our bodies, in our feelings, in our minds, and in the world. Each day thousands of children die of hunger. Plant and animal species are going extinct every day. Yet the sunrise is beautiful, and the rose that bloomed this morning along the wall is a miracle. Life is both dreadful and wonderful. To practice meditation is to be in touch with both aspects of life.

DON'T WASTE YOUR LIFE

On the wooden board outside of the meditation hall in many Zen monasteries, there is a four-line inscription. The last line is, "Do not squander your life." Our lives are made of days and hours, and each hour is precious. Have we wasted our hours and our days? Are we wasting our lives? When we practice sitting or walking meditation, it's easier to be mindful and concentrated. During the rest of the day, we also practice. It's more difficult, but it's possible. The sitting and the walking can be extended to the non-walking, non-sitting moments of our day. That is the basic principle of meditation.

HAPPINESS AND AWARENESS

Please do not think we must be solemn in order to meditate. Whether or not we are happy depends on our awareness. When you have a toothache, you think that not having a toothache will make you very happy. But when you don't have a toothache, often you are still not happy. All of us have the capacity of transforming neutral feelings into pleasant feelings. If you're rested and relaxed, all living beings will profit from your relaxation and energy. This is the most basic kind of peace work.

SMILING

A smile can relax hundreds of muscles in your face, and relax your nervous system. A smile makes you master of yourself. All day long, we can practice smiling. At first you may find it difficult to smile, and we have to think about why. Smiling means that we are ourselves, that we have sovereignty over ourselves, that we are not drowned in forgetfulness. I'd like to offer a short poem you can recite from time to time, while breathing and smiling:

Breathing in, I calm my body.
Breathing out, I smile.
Dwelling in the present moment,
I know this is a wonderful moment.

CALMING

"Breathing in, I calm my body." Reciting this line is like drinking a glass of cool water—you feel the freshness permeate your body. When I breathe in and recite this line, I actually feel the breathing calming my body, calming my mind.

PRESENT MOMENT, WONDERFUL MOMENT

While I sit here, I don't long to be somewhere else; I'm not pulled away by the future or by the past. I sit here, and I know where I am. This is very important. We tend to be alive in the future, not now. We say, "Wait until I finish school and get my PhD; then I'll really be living." Once we have it—and it wasn't easy to get—we say to ourselves, "I have to wait until I have a job for my life to really begin." Then after the job a car, and after the car a house. We aren't capable of being alive in the present moment. We tend to postpone being alive to the future, the distant future, we don't know when. It's as if now is not the moment to be alive. We may never be alive at all in our entire life. The only moment to be alive is in the present moment.

SELF-HEALING

We have to believe in our body's capacity to heal itself. The power of self-healing is a reality, but many of us don't believe in it. Instead, we take a lot of vitamins and medicines that may sometimes be harmful to our body. Taking good care of our bodies, eating well but not too much, sleeping, and drinking water, we have to trust the power of understanding, healing, and loving within us. It is our refuge. If we lose our faith and confidence in it, we lose everything. Instead of panicking or giving ourselves up to despair, we practice mindful breathing and put our trust in the healing power within us. We call this the island within ourselves in which we can take refuge. It is an island of peace, confidence, solidity, love, and freedom. Be that island for yourself. You

don't have to look elsewhere. Mindful breathing helps you go back to that precious island
within, so that you can experience the foundation of your being.

THE WAR INSIDE

We know that many of us don't want to go home to ourselves. We're afraid. There's a lot of internal suffering and conflict that we want to avoid. We complain that we don't have time to live, yet we try to kill our free time by not going back to ourselves. We escape by turning on the television or picking up a novel or a magazine; or we go out for a drive. We run away from ourselves and don't attend to our body, feelings, or states of mind. We have to go home. If we're at war with our parents, friends, society, or our church, it may be because there's a war raging within us. An internal war facilitates other wars. We're afraid of going home because we lack the tools or the means for self-protection. Equipped with mindfulness, we can go home safely and not be overwhelmed by our pain, sorrow, and depression. With some training, with the practice of mindful walking and mindful breathing, we'll be able to go home and embrace our pain and sorrow.

WATER OVER THE ROCKS

The activities of our mind, often unstable and agitated, are like a torrent of water washing over the rocks. In traditional Buddhist literature, the mind is often compared to a monkey always swinging from branch to branch or to a horse galloping out of control. Once our mind is able to identify what is happening, we will be able to see clearly our mental state and make it calm. Just that will bring us peace, joy, and stillness.

BOAT IN A STORM

Suppose you're on a boat crossing the ocean.
If you get caught in a storm, it's important to
stay calm and not panic. To accomplish that,
go back to your breathing and be yourself.
When you're calm, truly your own island, you
will know what to do and what not to do.
Otherwise, the boat may capsize. We destroy
ourselves by doing things we ought not to do.
Take refuge in mindfulness, and you will see
things more clearly and know how to improve
the situation. Mindfulness brings about concentration, and concentration brings about
insight and wisdom. This is the safest refuge.
The safety and stability your island can provide depend on your practice. Everything—
comforting a child, building a house, or playing
volleyball—depends on your practice.

ALL IS NOT SUFFERING

There are those who say that everything is suffering. This is not true. It's an exaggeration and a misunderstanding of what the Buddha said. The Buddha said that there is suffering, but he didn't say that's all there is. There are causes that bring about suffering, and it's possible to arrive at a state of the absence of these causes. Of course we shouldn't dream that one day we'll have one hundred percent happiness and not a single drop of suffering. There is always something. But we can handle suffering and happiness in an artful way.

RELEASING TENSION

The way to release all the tension is with our mindful breath. So we always start with mindfulness. Mindfulness brings the mind to the present moment, and we see and experience things more deeply. Going back to the present moment, you can see if your body is tense. We look deeply and see that, "Ah, I am tense because I'm carried away by my worry, anxiety, and plans." Then we can make the determination not to be carried away like that.

DESIRE AND HAPPINESS

The Buddha often said that many people confuse desire with happiness. Before he became a monk, the Buddha had grown up as a prince and had tasted a life of trying to satisfy desires, so his words came from experience. He said that true happiness is a life with few desires, few possessions, and the time to enjoy the many wonders in us and around us. Desire means to be caught in unwholesome longing. When the mind is desiring, we are aware of the presence of that state of mind. "This is the mind longing for wealth." "This is the mind desiring reputation." When the mind isn't desiring, it's important to observe that the desiring mind is not present. "This is the sense of ease that accompanies the absence of a mind desiring wealth." "This is the sense of ease that accompanies the absence of a mind desiring reputation," etc. We can experience happiness, ease, and peace when we observe these moments of no desire. Desirelessness is the basic condition that makes possible the feelings of joy, peace, and ease that come with living a simple life. Simplicity means to have few desires, to be content with a simple life and just a few possessions. Desirelessness is the basis of true happiness, because in true happiness there must be the elements of peace, joy, and ease.

RELAXING WHERE WE ARE

Living in the city, we may be very busy, and the city is very noisy and polluted. We can never see the moon or the stars, and we get caught in the city. We want to have a two-day vacation to leave the city and go to the countryside, but we can't go because we're not able to let go. One day a friend comes and says, "This Friday let's go to the countryside." That person is really good at convincing us to leave, so we accept. We get in the car, and after only forty-five minutes we have left the city behind and we can see the countryside. We feel the breeze, we see the spaciousness, and it gives us joy. That joy comes from being able to let go and leave the city behind. Letting go gives rise to joy and happiness. We need to

sit down with a piece of paper and write down
the things we can let go of. We're still caught
in many things. We're not happy and joyful,
because we haven't been able to let go.

IDEAS OF HAPPINESS

In order to be happy, we need first of all to let go of our ideas of happiness. It's difficult. Each one of us has an idea of happiness; we think that we must have this or that to be happy, or that we have to eliminate this or that to be happy. We think that we have to have certain conditions: We have to have this house or this car or that person to live with us so that we can be happy. We have these ideas of happiness. If we haven't been able to be happy and joyful, it's because we're caught in our ideas. So we have to be able to let them go. Our idea of happiness is the main obstacle to happiness.

NO COWS TO LOSE

One day the Buddha was sitting having a silent lunch together with his monks in the woods. A farmer came hurrying by and asked, "Dear monks, have you seen my cows? They have all left me this morning. If I don't have my cows, how can I live? Insects have eaten my fields of sesame; I couldn't harvest anything. I cannot live. I think I will kill myself." The Buddha said, "Dear friend, we've been sitting here for a while, and we haven't seen any cows pass by. Maybe you can look in another direction." So the farmer left. The Buddha turned to his monks and said, "Dear monks, you are very lucky. You don't have any cows to lose." A cow stands for something we need to let go of. Our idea of happiness is a cow. And it's because of this idea of happiness that we cannot be happy.

NAMING OUR COWS

Each one of us needs to sit down with a piece of paper and write down the names of all our cows. Among them are our ideas of happiness. We get caught and we suffer. We struggle with all these things, but we don't have the capacity to let them go. How many cows do we have? Sometimes we see that one page is not enough for us to write the names of all our cows. The truth is, if you let go of these cows, you will be lighter, and your happiness will be much greater. Let go so that happiness, joy, and peace can be possible.

OUR PEACE IS WHAT IS
MOST PRECIOUS

Awakening is something that happens today, not in ten or twenty years. Insights can come continuously to give us the understanding we need to untangle ourselves from attachments. When our mind is entangled with anger, jealousy, or sadness, we can be in that state hour after hour, day after day. It's a pity, because meanwhile, life is wondrous. If we only concentrate on breathing in and seeing that our body is a wonder, we can see that nothing else is really important. It's only the peace in our body and in our mind that matters. Anyone can attain this insight. While we sit, we can be with our breathing, we can let go of tensions, and we can have peace. This peace is the most precious thing there is, more precious than any pursuit.

FREEDOM IS A PRACTICE

If you want to be free, just concentrate on your in-breath and out-breath. Breathe in and out for three minutes, and in those three minutes you are free. This freedom is something we have to train ourselves to have. It's not something that comes automatically. When we have freedom, when we're not overwhelmed by anger or anxiety, then we can make the determination to practice cultivating this freedom. When we're anxious, worried, or angry, we can't make good decisions. When we're free, we make better decisions. This freedom is something we can attain whenever we like with the practice of breathing in mindfulness, walking in mindfulness.

DON'T BE TOO BUSY

As you go about your daily activities, do you feel you're lacking something? As you wash the dishes, cook a meal, clean the kitchen, while you walk, stand, sit, or lie down, what are you looking for? There's no business for you to take care of. You're free; there's nothing to do or to run after. Perhaps you're seeking something, calculating, or feeling agitated. Your feet and hands may always think they have to be doing something. When you do sitting or walking meditation, don't put too much effort into it. You're not trying to attain something. Meditation shouldn't be hard labor. The principle is to be ordinary, not to be too busy. We just live in a normal way. When we eat, we just eat; we don't speak. If we need to urinate, we urinate. If we're tired, then we can rest.

COMPASSION FOR YOURSELF

Don't consider anger, hatred, and greed as enemies you have to fight, destroy, or annihilate. If you annihilate anger, you annihilate yourself. Dealing with anger in that way would be like transforming yourself into a battlefield, and tearing yourself to bits. If you struggle in that way, you do violence to yourself. If you can't be compassionate to yourself, you won't be able to be compassionate to others. When we get angry, we have to produce awareness: "I am angry. Anger is in me. I am anger." That is the first thing to do.

Breathing in, I feel my anger.
Breathing out, I smile.
I stay with my breathing
so I won't lose myself.

NO BLAMING

When you plant a tree, if it doesn't grow well,
you don't blame the tree. You look into the
reasons it isn't doing well. It may need fertilizer
or more water or less sun. We never blame the
tree. Yet we're quick to blame our child. If we
know how to take care of her, she will grow
well, like a tree. Blaming has no good effect
at all. Never blame, never try to persuade
using reason and arguments; they never lead
to any positive effect. That is my experience.
No argument, no reasoning, no blaming, just
understanding. If you understand, and you
show that you understand, you can love, and
the situation will change.

THE BREATH IS A BRIDGE

Our breath is like a bridge connecting body and mind. In our daily lives, our bodies may be in one place and our minds somewhere else, in the past, or in the future. This is called a state of distraction. The breath is a connection between the body and the mind. When you begin to breathe in and out mindfully, your mind will come back to your body. You will be able to realize the oneness of body and mind and become fully present and fully alive in the here and the now. You will be in a position to touch life deeply in this moment. This isn't something difficult. Everyone can do it.

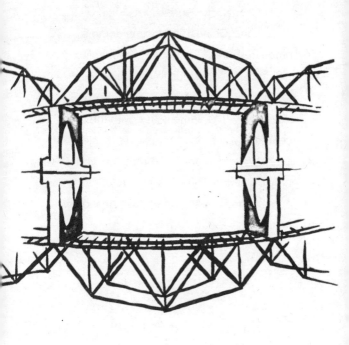

RELAXED PRACTICE

In traditional Chinese medicine, doctors sometimes offer their patients something healing that is delicious to eat. Just by eating, you begin to heal in a pleasant and relaxed way. The same is true with the practice. While you practice sitting, you enjoy sitting. While you practice breathing, you enjoy breathing. If you are able to enjoy yourself, then healing and transformation will take place.

LIBERATION

We often live as if we're in a dream. We're dragged into the past or pulled into the future. We're bound by our sorrow, agitation, and fear. We hold on to our anger, which blocks communication. "Liberation" means transforming and transcending these conditions in order to be fully awake, at ease, peaceful, joyful, and fresh. We practice stopping and observing deeply in order to arrive at liberation. When we live in this way, our life is worth living, and we become a source of joy to our family and to everyone around us.

RELAXED SITTING

When you sit and watch television, you don't make any effort. That's why you can sit there for a long time. When you sit in meditation, if you struggle, you won't be able to sit for very long. Please imitate the way you sit in your living room. Effortlessness is the key to success. Don't fight. Don't try hard. Just allow yourself to sit. This relaxing way of sitting is also restful. Allow your body to rest and be at ease.

SETTLING DOWN

When you pour fresh juice into a glass and let it stand for fifteen minutes, all the pulp sinks down to the bottom of the glass. If you allow yourself to sit in a relaxed, peaceful way, it calms and settles your body and your mind. Sitting like this allows you to enjoy your in-breath and out-breath, to enjoy being alive, to enjoy just sitting there.

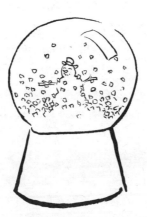

THE HABIT OF TENSION

A number of years ago, I went to India to visit
the Buddhist community of untouchables. A
friend had organized the teaching tour for me.
He belonged to that caste, which has been
discriminated against for so many thousands
of years. He was sitting next to me in the bus,
on my right. I was enjoying looking out the
window and seeing the countryside of India.
But when I looked at him, I saw that he was
very tense. He had done everything to make
my visit pleasant, yet he continued to worry.
This habit energy had been transmitted to
him from many generations of ancestors who
had struggled all their lives against discrimination. It's hard to transform that kind of habit. I
said, "Dear friend, why are you so tense? You

have arranged everything beautifully. There's nothing to do now that we're here on the bus; and when we arrive, our friends will come to the station to meet us. Sit back and relax and enjoy the countryside." He said, "Okay," but just two minutes later, he looked exactly as before, very tense, worrying about the future, and not being able to be at ease in the here and now. So many of us are like that. Our practice is to stop running, and to be aware that all the wonders of life are available in the here and now.

MEDITATIONS
FOR RESTING
AND RELAXING

INVITING THE BELL

There is tranquility, peace, and joy within us, but we have to call them forth so they can manifest. Inviting a bell to sound is one way to call forth the joy and tranquility within. I have been inviting the bell since I was sixteen. When I want to invite the small bell, I hold it in the palm of my hand and I breathe in and out. "Breathing in, I calm myself. Breathing out, I smile." If you want to invite the bell, here is a short poem to learn by heart. Recite the first line of the poem as you breathe in, the second line as you breathe out, and so on:

Body, speech, and mind in perfect oneness,
I send my heart along with the sound of this bell.
May all the hearers awaken from forgetfulness,
and transcend the path of anxiety and sorrow.

LISTENING TO THE BELL

The bell is a friend, someone who helps us come back to ourselves and become calm. We invite tranquility to manifest. With the help of the bell, our mind is collected and brought back to the present moment. We stop our thinking and talking and come back to ourselves, breathing and relaxing. As you listen, you may notice that your in-breath and out-breath naturally become longer and more relaxed. Here is a poem for listening to the bell. "Your true home" means your own island, your solidity, peace, and joy.

Listen, listen.
This wonderful sound
brings me back
to my true home.

EASING WORRY

Sometimes we think and worry nonstop. It's like having a cassette tape continually turning in our minds. When we leave the television set on for a long time, it becomes hot. Our head also gets hot from all our thinking. When we can't stop, we may be unable to sleep well. Even if we take a sleeping pill, we continue to run, think, and worry in our dreams. The alternative medicine is mindful breathing. If we practice mindful breathing for five minutes, allowing our body to rest, then we stop thinking for that time. We can use words like "in" and "out" to help us be aware of our breathing. This is not thinking; these words aren't concepts. They're guides for mindfulness of breathing. When we think too much, the quality of our being is reduced. Stopping the

thinking, we increase the quality of our being.
There's more peace, relaxation, and rest.

IN, OUT. DEEP, SLOW.

Here is a poem to practice any time, but especially when you're angry, worried, or sad. If you know how to practice this poem, you'll feel much better after just one or two minutes.

> In, Out.
> Deep, Slow.
> Calm, Ease.
> Smile, Release.
> Present Moment, Wonderful Moment.

"In, Out," means that when I breathe in, I know I'm breathing in, and when I breathe out, I know I'm breathing out. You are one-hundred percent with your in-breath and your out-breath. Don't think of anything else. That's the secret of success.

After you've practiced "In, Out" three, four, or five times, you'll notice that your in-breath naturally becomes deeper, and your out-breath becomes slower. Your breath is calm, and you're more peaceful. That is "Deep, Slow."

"Calm, Ease" means, "Breathing in, I feel calm. Breathing out, I feel at ease." This exercise is wonderful to practice, especially when you're nervous, or angry, or you don't feel peaceful in yourself.

Then you come to "Smile, Release." "Breathing in, I smile." You may feel it's too difficult to smile. But after practicing three or four times, you may feel that you're able to smile. If you can smile, you'll feel a lot better. You may protest, "Why do you want me to smile? It's not natural." Many people ask me that and they protest, "I have no joy in me. I can't force myself to smile; it wouldn't be true." I always say that a smile can be a kind of yoga practice, yoga of the mouth. You just smile, even if you don't feel joy. And after you smile, you'll see you feel differently. Sometimes the mind takes the initiative, and sometimes you have to allow the body to take the initiative.

BODY SCAN

If you only have a few minutes to sit or lie down and relax, you can do a body scan. Beginning at the top of your head and moving down to your toes, you bring mindful awareness to parts of your body. You can bring attention to many or just a few parts of your body. This can be done anytime, anywhere to rest and relieve stress in body and mind.

Breathing in, I am aware of my eyes.
Breathing out, I smile to my eyes.

Having eyes in good condition is a wonderful thing. We need to take care of our eyes and rest them from time to time, especially when we're working.

Breathing in, I am aware of my heart.
Breathing out, I smile to my heart.

You have neglected your heart for a long time. You may cause trouble for your heart by the way you rest, work, eat, and drink. Your heart works day and night for your well-being, but because of your lack of mindfulness, you have not been very helpful to your heart. Once or twice each day, you can pick at least one part of your body to focus on and practice relaxing.

TELEPHONE MEDITATION

When you want to pick up the phone to call someone, first practice breathing in and out to calm yourself.

Words can travel thousands of miles.
Words can help restore communication
and build mutual understanding.
I vow that the conversation I'm going to have
will bring us closer together,
and make our friendship bloom like a flower.

When you receive a call, you can also practice mindful breathing before answering the phone.

I listen, I listen.
The mindfulness bell of the telephone
brings me back to my true home.

COMPUTER MEDITATION

A bell is a friend, an invention to help us. If you work on a computer, you might get so carried away by your work that you forget you have a body; you forget that you're alive. You even forget to breathe sometimes. So you may like to program your computer so that every quarter of an hour it offers the sound of the bell, enabling you to go back to yourself, to smile, and to breathe in and out before you continue working. Many of us have done that. The sound of a bell reminding you to come back to yourself and enjoy breathing is a wonderful way to take a break.

DEEP RELAXATION

Deep relaxation is an opportunity for your body to rest, heal, and be restored. You bring attention to each part of your body: hair, scalp, brain, ears, neck, shoulders, arms, hands, fingers, lungs, each of the internal organs, the digestive system, pelvis, legs, feet, toes. You send your love and care to every part of your body and every cell.

Lie down on your back with your arms at your sides. Make yourself comfortable. Allow your body to relax. Be aware of the floor beneath you and the contact of your body with the floor. Allow your body to sink into the floor.

Become aware of your breathing, in and out. Be aware of your abdomen rising and falling as you breathe in and out.

Breathing in, bring your awareness to your eyes. Breathing out, allow your eyes to relax. Allow your eyes to sink back into your head. Let go of the tension in all the tiny muscles around your eyes. Your eyes allow you to see a paradise of forms and colors. Allow your eyes to rest. Send love and gratitude to your eyes.

Breathing in, bring your awareness to your mouth. Breathing out, allow your mouth to relax. Release the tension around your mouth. Your lips are the petals of a flower. Let a gentle smile bloom on your lips. Smiling releases the tension in the hundreds of muscles in your face. Feel the tension release in your cheeks, your jaw, and your throat.

Breathing in, bring your awareness to your shoulders. Breathing out, allow your shoulders to relax. Let them sink into the floor. Let all the accumulated tension flow into the floor. You carry so much with your shoulders. Now let your shoulders relax as you care for them.

Breathing in, become aware of your arms. Breathing out, relax your arms. Let your arms sink into the floor. Relax your upper arms, your elbows, your lower arms, your wrists, your hands, and all the tiny muscles in your fingers. Move your fingers a little if you need to, helping the muscles relax.

Breathing in, bring your awareness to your heart. Breathing out, allow your heart to relax.

You have neglected your heart for a long time, and you cause your heart stress by the way you work, eat, and manage anxiety and stress. Your heart beats for you night and day. Embrace your heart with mindfulness and tenderness, reconciling and taking care of your heart.

Breathing in, bring your awareness to your legs. Breathing out, allow your legs to relax. Release all the tension in your legs, your thighs, your knees, your calves, your ankles, your feet, your toes, and all the tiny muscles in your toes. You may want to move your toes a little to help them relax. Send your love and care to your toes.

Breathing in, breathing out, your whole body feels as light as a lily floating on the water. You have nowhere to go, nothing to do. You are free as a cloud floating in the sky.

Bring your awareness back to your breathing, to your abdomen rising and falling.

Following your breathing, become aware of your arms and legs. You may want to move them a little and stretch.

When you feel ready, slowly sit up.

When you are ready, slowly stand up.

RELATED TITLES

Awakening Joy · James Baraz and Shoshana Alexander

Be Free Where You Are · Thich Nhat Hanh

Breathe, You Are Alive! · Thich Nhat Hanh

Deep Relaxation · Sister Chan Khong

Happiness · Thich Nhat Hanh

How to Eat · Thich Nhat Hanh

How to Love · Thich Nhat Hanh

How to Sit · Thich Nhat Hanh

The Long Road Turns to Joy · Thich Nhat Hanh

Making Space · Thich Nhat Hanh

Not Quite Nirvana · Rachel Neumann

Planting Seeds · Thich Nhat Hanh and the Plum Village Community

Ten Breaths to Happiness · Glen Schneider

World As Lover, World As Self · Joanna Macy

Monastics and visitors practice the art of mindful living in the tradition of Thich Nhat Hanh at our ten mindfulness practice centers around the world. For a full listing of practice centers, or for information about retreats, visit plumvillage.org or contact:

Plum Village
33580 Dieulivol, France
plumvillage.org

Deer Park Monastery
Escondido, CA 92026, USA
deerparkmonastery.org

Magnolia Grove Monastery
Batesville, MS 38606, USA
magnoliagrovemonastery.org

Blue Cliff Monastery
Pine Bush, NY 12566, USA
bluecliffmonastery.org

European Institute of
Applied Buddhism
D-51545 Waldbröl, Germany
eiab.eu

Thailand Plum Village
Nakhon Ratchasima,
30130 Thailand
phfhk.org

The Mindfulness Bell, a journal of the art of mindful living in the tradition of Thich Nhat Hanh, is published three times a year by our community. To subscribe or to see the worldwide directory of Sanghas, or local mindfulness groups, visit mindfulnessbell.org.

The Thich Nhat Hanh Foundation supports Thich Nhat Hanh's peace work and mindfulness teachings around the world. For more information on how you can help or on how to nourish your mindfulness practice, visit the foundation at tnhf.org.

PARALLAX PRESS

Parallax Press, a nonprofit publisher founded by
Zen Master Thich Nhat Hanh, publishes books
and media on the art of mindful living and
Engaged Buddhism. We are committed to offering
teachings that help transform suffering and
injustice. Our aspiration is to contribute to collective
insight and awakening, bringing about a more
joyful, healthy, and compassionate society.

View our entire library at **parallax.org**.

HOW TO LOVE

LOVE

THICH NHAT HANH

**PARALLAX
PRESS**

BERKELEY, CALIFORNIA

Parallax Press
P.O. Box 7355
Berkeley, California 94707
www.parallax.org

Parallax Press is the publishing division of
Plum Village Community of Engaged Buddhism, Inc.
Copyright © 2015 Plum Village Community of
Engaged Buddhism, Inc.
All rights reserved

Printed by Friesens, Altona, MB, Canada, employee owned
and operated

Cover and text design by Debbie Berne
Illustrations by Jason DeAntonis

ISBN: 978-1-937006-88-4

Library of Congress Cataloging-in-Publication Data

Nhat Hanh, Thich, author.
 How to love / Thich Nhat Hanh.
    pages cm
 Includes bibliographical references.
 ISBN 978-1-937006-88-4
1. Love—Religious aspects—Buddhism. 2. Buddhism—
Spiritual life. I. Title.
 BQ9800.T5392N45449 2015
 294.3'5677—dc23

                                    2014041483

12 / 22

CONTENTS

NOTES ON LOVE

HEART LIKE A RIVER

If you pour a handful of salt into a cup of water, the water becomes undrinkable. But if you pour the salt into a river, people can continue to draw the water to cook, wash, and drink. The river is immense, and it has the capacity to receive, embrace, and transform. When our hearts are small, our understanding and compassion are limited, and we suffer. We can't accept or tolerate others and their shortcomings, and we demand that they change. But when our hearts expand, these same things don't make us suffer anymore. We have a lot of understanding and compassion and can embrace others. We accept others as they are, and then they have a chance to transform. So the big question is: how do we help our hearts to grow?

FEEDING OUR LOVE

Each of us can learn the art of nourishing
happiness and love. Everything needs food
to live, even love. If we don't know how to
nourish our love, it withers. When we feed and
support our own happiness, we are nourishing
our ability to love. That's why to love means to
learn the art of nourishing our happiness.

UNDERSTANDING IS THE NATURE OF LOVE

Understanding someone's suffering is the best gift you can give another person. Understanding is love's other name. If you don't understand, you can't love.

RECOGNIZING TRUE LOVE

True love gives us beauty, freshness, solidity, freedom, and peace. True love includes a feeling of deep joy that we are alive. If we don't feel this way when we feel love, then it's not true love.

REVERENCE IS THE NATURE
OF OUR LOVE

There's a tradition in Asia of treating your partner with the respect you would accord a guest.
This is true even if you have been with your
loved one for a long time. The other person
always deserves your full respect. Reverence
is the nature of our love.

LOVE IS EXPANSIVE

In the beginning of a relationship, your love may include only you and the other person. But if you practice true love, very soon that love will grow and include all of us. The moment love stops growing, it begins to die. It's like a tree; if a tree stops growing, it begins to die. We can learn how to feed our love and help it continue to grow.

LOVE IS ORGANIC

Love is a living, breathing thing. There is no need to force it to grow in a particular direction. If we start by being easy and gentle with ourselves, we will find it is just there inside of us, solid and healing.

DISTRACTIONS

Often, we get crushes on others not because we truly love and understand them, but to distract ourselves from our suffering. When we learn to love and understand ourselves and have true compassion for ourselves, then we can truly love and understand another person.

THE FOUR ELEMENTS OF
TRUE LOVE

True love is made of four elements: loving
kindness, compassion, joy, and equanimity. In
Sanskrit, these are, *maitri, karuna, mudita,* and
upeksha. If your love contains these elements,
it will be healing and transforming, and it will
have the element of holiness in it. True love
has the power to heal and transform any
situation and bring deep meaning to our lives.

LOVING KINDNESS

The first element of true love is loving kindness. The essence of loving kindness is being able to offer happiness. You can be the sunshine for another person. You can't offer happiness until you have it for yourself. So build a home inside by accepting yourself and learning to love and heal yourself. Learn how to practice mindfulness in such a way that you can create moments of happiness and joy for your own nourishment. Then you have something to offer the other person.

COMPASSION

The second element of true love is compassion. Compassion is the capacity to understand the suffering in oneself and in the other person. If you understand your own suffering, you can help him to understand his suffering. Understanding suffering brings compassion and relief. You can transform your own suffering and help transform the suffering of the other person with the practice of mindfulness and looking deeply.

JOY

The third element of true love is the capacity to offer joy. When you know how to generate joy, it nourishes you and nourishes the other person. Your presence is an offering, like fresh air, or spring flowers, or the bright blue sky.

EQUANIMITY

The fourth element of true love is equanimity. We can also call it inclusiveness or nondiscrimination. In a deep relationship, there's no longer a boundary between you and the other person. You are her and she is you. Your suffering is her suffering. Your understanding of your own suffering helps your loved one to suffer less. Suffering and happiness are no longer individual matters. What happens to your loved one happens to you. What happens to you happens to your loved one.

RESPECT AND TRUST

Along with the traditional four elements of true love—loving kindness, compassion, joy, and equanimity—there are two more elements: respect and trust. These elements can be found in the four, but it helps to mention their names. When you love someone, you have to have trust and confidence. Love without trust is not yet love. Of course, first you have to have trust, respect, and confidence in yourself. Trust that you have a good and compassionate nature. You are part of the universe; you are made of stars. When you look at your loved one, you see that he is also made of stars and carries eternity inside. Looking in this way, we naturally feel reverence. True love cannot be without trust and respect for oneself and for the other person.

BE BEAUTIFUL, BE YOURSELF

If you can accept your body, then you have a chance to see your body as your home. You can rest in your body, settle in, relax, and feel joy and ease. If you don't accept your body and your mind, you can't be at home with yourself. You have to accept yourself as you are. This is a very important practice. As you practice building a home in yourself, you become more and more beautiful.

YOU ARE A FLOWER

Every child is born in the garden of humanity as a flower. Each flower differs from every other flower. There are many messages in our society that tell us, even when we're young people, that there's something wrong with us and that if we just buy the right product, or look a certain way, or have the right partner, that will fix it. As grown-ups, we can remind young people that they're already beautiful as they are; they don't have to be someone else.

WATERING THE FLOWER
IN A FRIEND

One day I was giving a talk at our practice center in France. Two of the people in attendance were a couple from Bordeaux who visit our center on occasion. The woman was sitting in the front of the audience, and she was crying from the beginning of the talk to the end. After the talk I went to her husband and told him, "Dear friend, your flower needs some water." He understood right away. After lunch, they drove home through the countryside, and he spent that hour and a half letting her know all the things he appreciated about her. When they arrived home, their children were surprised to see their mother and father so joyful. Transformation can happen very quickly.

HUGGING

In 1966, a friend took me to the Atlanta Airport. When we were saying good-bye she asked, "Is it all right to hug a Buddhist monk?" In my country, we're not used to expressing ourselves that way, but I thought, "I'm a Zen teacher. It should be no problem for me to do that." So I said, "Why not?" and she hugged me, but I was quite stiff. While on the plane, I decided that if I wanted to work with friends in the West, I would have to learn the culture of the West. So I invented hugging meditation. Hugging meditation is a combination of East and West. According to the practice, you have to really hug the person you are holding. You have to make him or her very real in your arms, not just for the sake of appearances, patting him on the back to pretend you are there, but breathing consciously and hugging with all your body, spirit, and heart. Hugging meditation is a practice of mindfulness. "Breathing in, I know my dear one is in my arms, alive. Breathing out, she is so precious to me." If you breathe deeply like that, holding the person you love, the energy of your care and appreciation will penetrate into that person and she will be nourished and bloom like a flower.

BODY AND MIND

Body and mind are not two separate entities. What happens in the body will have an effect on the mind and vice versa. Mind relies on the body to manifest, and body relies on mind in order to be alive, in order to be possible. When you love someone, you have to respect her, not only her mind but also her body. You respect your own body, and you respect her body. Your body is you. Your body is your mind. The other person's mind and body are also connected.

SPIRITUAL PRACTICE

Spirituality doesn't mean a blind belief in a spiritual teaching. Spirituality is a practice that brings relief, communication, and transformation. Everyone needs a spiritual dimension in life. Without a spiritual dimension, it's very challenging to be with the daily difficulties we all encounter. With a spiritual practice, you're no longer afraid. Along with your physical body, you have a spiritual body. The practices of breathing, walking, concentration, and understanding can help you greatly in dealing with your emotions, in listening to and embracing your suffering, and in helping you to recognize and embrace the suffering of another person. If we have this capacity, then we can develop a real and lasting spiritual intimacy with ourselves and with others.

THREE KINDS OF INTIMACY

There are three kinds of intimacy: physical, emotional, and spiritual. These three should go together. Every one of us is seeking emotional intimacy. We want to have real communication, mutual understanding, and communion. We want to be in harmony with someone. When an intimate relationship contains all three elements, then physical intimacy is more meaningful and can be very healthy and healing.

EMPTY SEX

Sexual desire is not love. Sexual activity without love is called empty sex. If you satisfy your body but don't satisfy your heart and your mind, are you satisfied? Do you feel whole and connected? When your body, heart, and mind are satisfied, sexual intimacy connects you more deeply with yourself and your partner.

SAYING "NO"

Loving someone doesn't mean saying "yes" to whatever the other person wants. The basis of loving someone else is to know yourself and to know what you need. I know a woman who suffered very much because she couldn't say "no." From the time she was young, whenever a man asked her for something, she felt she had to say "yes" even when she didn't want to. It's important that loving another person doesn't take priority over listening to yourself and knowing what you need.

THREE STRONG ROOTS

To keep our commitment to our partner, and to weather the most difficult storms, we need strong roots. If we wait until there is trouble with our partner to try and solve it, we won't have built strong enough roots to withstand the assault. Often we think we're balanced when, in reality, that balance is fragile. We only need a slight breeze to blow for us to fall down. A juniper tree has its roots planted deep in the heart of the earth. As a result it is solid and strong. But some trees that appear to be quite steady, need only one raging storm to knock them down. Resilient trees can weather a violent storm because their roots are deep and firm. The roots of a lasting relationship are mindfulness, deep listening and loving speech, and a strong community to support you.

SHARING THE
SAME ASPIRATION

In a relationship, when you and your partner share the same kind of aspiration, you become one, and you become an instrument of love and peace in the world. You begin as a community of two people, and then you can grow your community. In the practice center where I live, there are over a hundred of us. We have the same concerns, the same desires, and the same future. There is no longer a place for jealousy, because we are all faithful to the same aspiration. We share everything, but we still have our freedom intact. Love is not a kind of prison. True love gives us a lot of space.

LOVING COMMUNICATION

To love without knowing *how* to love wounds the person we love. To know how to love someone, we have to understand them. To understand, we need to listen. That person may be our partner, our friend, our sibling, or our child. You can ask, "Dear one, do you think that I understand you enough? Please tell me your difficulties, your suffering, and your deepest wishes." Then the other person has an opportunity to open their heart.

BREATHING TO AVOID AN ARGUMENT

Everyone knows that blaming and arguing
never help; but we forget. Conscious breathing
helps us develop the ability to stop at that
crucial moment, to keep ourselves from saying
or doing something we regret later. Practice
conscious breathing when things are going
well with your partner, then it will be there for
you when things get hard.

LISTENING WITH PATIENCE

When your loved one is talking, practice listening deeply. Sometimes the other person will say something that surprises us, that is the opposite of the way we see things. Allow the other person to speak freely. Don't cut your loved one off or criticize their words. When we listen deeply with all our heart—for ten minutes, half an hour, or even an hour—we will begin to see the other person more deeply and understand them better. If they say something that's incorrect, that's based on a wrong perception, we can give them a little information later on to help them correct their thinking. But right now, we just listen.

LIBERATION FROM COMPLEXES

Often we can't love ourselves or others fully when we're stuck in our own complexes. When you have an inferiority complex, you have low self-esteem, and this is a kind of sickness. High self-esteem is also a sickness, because you consider yourself to be above others and that causes suffering as well. Although equality is something good, it can also be a complex. When you say, "I'm as good as he is," you still think you have a separate self. When you compare two selves to each other, suffering will result. Real liberty is freedom from all these complexes.

A TRUE PARTNER

We tend to wonder if we have enough to offer
in a relationship. We're thirsty for truth, goodness, compassion, spiritual beauty, so we go
looking outside. Sometimes we think we've
found a partner who embodies all that is good,
beautiful, and true. After a time, we usually
discover that we've had a wrong perception of
that person, and we become disappointed. A
true partner or friend is one who encourages
you to look deep inside yourself for the beauty
and love you've been seeking.

JOY IS HEALING

If a relationship can't provide joy, then it's
not true love. If you keep making the other
person cry all day, that's not true love. Offer
only the things that can make the other person
happy. You should know the real needs of that
person. Practice and learn how to generate
a feeling of joy, a feeling of happiness with
your in-breath, your out-breath, and your
steps. If you have enough understanding and
love, then every moment—whether it's spent
making breakfast, driving the car, watering the
garden, or doing anything else in your day—
can be a moment of joy.

NOURISHED BY JOY

Learn to nourish yourself and the other person with joy. Are you able to make the other person smile? Are you able to increase her confidence and enthusiasm? If you're not able to do these small things for her, how can you say you love her? Sometimes a kind word is enough to help someone blossom like a flower.

ATTENTION

As long as we're rejecting ourselves and causing harm to our bodies and minds, there's no point in talking about loving and accepting others. With mindfulness, we can recognize our habitual ways of thinking and the contents of our thoughts. Sometimes our thoughts run around in circles and we're engulfed in distrust, pessimism, conflict, sorrow, or jealousy. This state of mind will naturally manifest in our words and actions and cause harm to us and to others. When we shed the light of mindfulness on our habitual thought patterns, we see them clearly. Recognizing our habits and smiling to them is the practice of appropriate mental attention, which helps us create new and more beneficial neural pathways.

LOVER AS HEALER

The Sanskrit word *karuna* is often translated as "compassion." Compassion means to "suffer with" another person, to share their suffering. Karuna is much more than that. It's the capacity to remove and transform suffering, not just to share it. When you go to a doctor, it doesn't help if she just shares your suffering. A doctor has to help heal the suffering. When you love someone, you should have the capacity to bring relief and help him to suffer less. This is an art. If you don't understand the roots of his suffering, you can't help, just as a doctor can't help heal your illness if she doesn't know the cause. You need to understand the cause of your loved one's suffering in order to help bring relief.

LOVING MINDFULLY

"Love" is a beautiful word, and we have to restore its meaning. When we say, "I love hamburgers," we spoil the word. We have to make the effort to heal words by using them properly and carefully. True love includes a sense of responsibility and accepting the other person as she is, with all her strengths and weaknesses. If you only like the best things in a person, that is not love. You have to accept her weaknesses and bring your patience, understanding, and energy to help her transform. This kind of love brings protection and safety.

NONDISCRIMINATION

In true love, there's no more separation or discrimination. His happiness is your happiness. Your suffering is his suffering. You can no longer say, "That's your problem." In true love, both happiness and suffering are no longer individual matters. You are him, and he is you. In a good relationship we are like two fingers of the same hand. The little finger doesn't suffer from an inferiority complex and say, "I'm so small. I wish I were as big as the thumb." The thumb doesn't have a superiority complex, saying, "I'm more important. I'm the big brother of all the fingers; you have to obey me." Instead, there's a perfect collaboration between them.

ASKING FOR HELP

When you suffer, you may want to go to your room, lock the door, and cry. The person who hurt you is the last person you want to see. Even if he tries to approach you, you may still be very angry. But to get relief, you have to go to the person you love, the one who just hurt you very deeply, and ask for help. Become yourself one hundred percent. Open your mouth and say with all your heart and with all your concentration that you suffer and you need help.

THREE HELPFUL SENTENCES

It's not healthy to keep anger inside for too
long. If you're too upset to speak calmly, you
can write a note and put it where the other
person will see it. Here are three sentences
that may help. First: "My dear, I am suffering, I
am angry, and I want you to know it." The second is: "I am doing my best." This means you
are practicing mindful breathing and walking,
and you are refraining from doing or saying
anything out of anger. The third is: "Please
help me." Memorize these sentences. Or write
them on a small piece of paper, the size of
a credit card, and put it in your wallet. Then
when you're angry, you can take it out, and
you will know exactly what to do.

ARE YOU SURE?

Other people's actions are the result of their own pain and not the result of any intention to hurt you. A wrong perception can be the cause of a lot of suffering. This is why, whenever we have a perception, we have to ask ourselves if our perception is right. When we stand with friends looking at the setting sun, we're sure the sun has not set quite yet. But a scientist might tell us that the sun we're seeing is only the image of the sun of eight minutes ago. We are subject to thousands of wrong perceptions like this in our daily lives. The next time you suffer, and you believe that your suffering has been caused by the person you love the most, ask your loved one for help.

PRIDE

Often, our pride stands in the way of our asking for help. In true love there is no place for pride. To love each other means to trust each other. If you don't tell the person you love of your suffering, it means you don't love this person enough to trust her. You have to realize that this person is the best person to help you. We need to be able to get help from the person we love.

REDISCOVERING APPRECIATION

When a loved one is suffering a lot, he or she doesn't have enough energy to embrace you and help you to suffer less. So it's natural that you become disappointed. You think that the other person's presence is no longer helpful to you. You may even wonder if you love this person anymore. If you're patient and you practice taking care of yourself and the other person, you may have a chance to discover that the elements of goodness and beauty in the person you love are still there. Taking care of yourself, you can support your loved one and reestablish the joy in your relationship.

A DEEP THIRST

Sometimes we feel empty; we feel a vacuum, a great lack of something. We don't know the cause; it's very vague, but that feeling of being empty inside is very strong. We expect and hope for something much better so we'll feel less alone, less empty. The desire to understand ourselves and to understand life is a deep thirst. There's also the deep thirst to be loved and to love. We are ready to love and be loved. It's very natural. But because we feel empty, we try to find an object of our love. Sometimes we haven't had the time to understand ourselves, yet we've already found the object of our love. When we realize that all our hopes and expectations of course can't be fulfilled by that person, we continue to feel empty. You want to find something, but you don't know what to search for. In everyone there's a continuous desire and expectation; deep inside, you still expect something better to happen. That is why you check your email many times a day!

A POT IN SEARCH OF A LID

Very often we feel like a pot without a lid. We believe that our lid is somewhere in the world and that if we look very hard, we'll find the right lid to cover our pot. The feeling of emptiness is always there inside us. When we contemplate the other person, sometimes we think we see what we feel we lack. We think we need someone else to lean on, to take refuge in, and to diminish our suffering. We want to be the object of another person's attention and contemplation. We want someone who will look at us and embrace our feeling of emptiness and suffering with his energy of mindfulness. Soon we become addicted to that kind of energy; we think that without that attention, we can't live. It helps us feel less empty and helps us forget the block of suffering inside. When we ourselves can't generate the energy to take care of ourselves, we think we need the energy of someone else. We focus on the need and the lack rather than generating the energy of mindfulness, concentration, and insight that can heal our suffering and help the other person as well.

BEFORE COMMITTING
TO ANOTHER

There was a couple who were about to get married in Plum Village, the practice center where I live. They wanted to see me before the wedding ceremony and I received them in my hut. They said, "Thay, there are only twenty-four hours left before our wedding. What do you think that we can do to prepare for our married life to be successful?" I said, "The most important thing for you to do is to look deeply into yourself, to see if there is something that is still an obstacle for you. Is there anyone with whom you haven't reconciled? Is there anything within you that you haven't reconciled with?" Reconciliation can also be with your own self. If you don't reconcile with yourself, happiness with another person is impossible.

RECONCILING FROM
A DISTANCE

Even if the person with whom you need to
reconcile is very far away, you can still do the
work of reconciliation now. What is important
is to reconcile within your own heart and mind.
If reconciliation is done within, that is enough.
Because the effect of that reconciliation will
be felt everywhere later on. Even if the person
you want to reconcile with refuses to respond,
or even if she's already dead, reconciliation
is still possible. Reconciliation means to work
it out within yourself so that peace can be
restored. Reconcile with yourself for the sake
of the world, for the sake of all living beings.
Your peace and serenity are crucial for all
of us.

STARTING A FAMILY

Before having a child, it would be wonderful if people would take a year to look deeply into themselves, to practice loving speech and deep listening, and to learn the other practices that will help them enjoy themselves and their children more. Bringing a new life into the world is a serious matter. Taking a year for introspection and preparation doesn't seem too much. Doctors and therapists spend up to ten years to get a license. But anyone can become a parent without any training or preparation. Parents can learn how to sow seeds of happiness, peace, and joy in the new child.

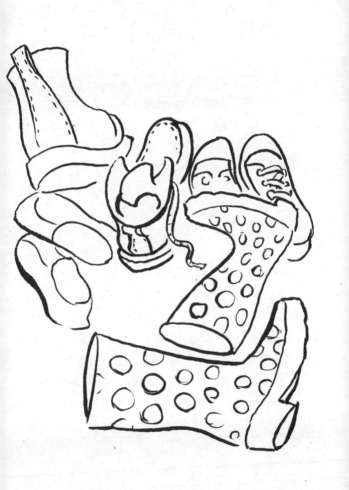

THE PRACTICE OF METTA

To love is, first of all, to accept ourselves as
we actually are. The first practice of love is
to know oneself. The Pali word *metta* means
"loving kindness." When we practice Metta
Meditation, we see the conditions that have
caused us to be the way we are; this makes it
easy for us to accept ourselves, including our
suffering and our happiness. When we practice Metta Meditation, we touch our deepest
aspirations. But the willingness and aspiration
to love is not yet love. We have to look deeply,
with all our being, in order to understand the
object of our meditation. The practice of love
meditation is not autosuggestion. We have to
look deeply at our body, feelings, perceptions,

mental formations, and consciousness. We can observe how much peace, happiness, and lightness we already have. We can notice whether we are anxious about accidents or misfortunes, and how much anger, irritation, fear, anxiety, or worry are still in us. As we become aware of the feelings in us, our self-understanding will deepen. We will see how our fears and lack of peace contribute to our unhappiness, and we will see the value of loving ourselves and cultivating a heart of compassion. Love will enter our thoughts, words, and actions.

DIGGING DEEP

Practicing loving kindness meditation is like digging deep into the ground until we reach the purest water. We look deeply into ourselves until insight arises and our love flows to the surface. Joy and happiness radiate from our eyes, and everyone around us benefits from our smile and our presence. If we take good care of ourselves, we help everyone. We stop being a source of suffering to the world, and we become a reservoir of joy and freshness. Here and there are people who know how to take good care of themselves, who live joyfully and happily. They are our strongest support. Whatever they do, they do for everyone.

MAKING MISTAKES

Since we're human beings, we make mistakes. We cause others to suffer. We hurt our loved ones, and we feel regret. But without making mistakes, there is no way to learn. If you can learn from your mistakes, then you have already transformed garbage into flowers. Very often, our mistakes come from our unskillfulness, and not because we want to harm one another. I think of our behavior in terms of being more or less skillful rather than in terms of good and bad. If you are skillful, you can avoid making yourself suffer and the other person suffer. If there's something you want to tell the other person, then you have to say it, but do so skillfully, in a way that leads to less rather than more suffering.

GOODWILL IS NOT ENOUGH

Your good intentions are not enough; you have
to be artful. We may be filled with goodwill;
we may be motivated by the desire to make
the other person happy; but out of our clumsi-
ness, we make them unhappy. Walking, eating,
breathing, talking, and working are all opportunities to practice creating happiness inside
you and around you. Mindful living is an art,
and each of us has to train to be an artist.

FINDING HOME

Every one of us is trying to find our true
home. Some of us are still searching. Our
true home is inside, but it's also in our loved
ones around us. When you're in a loving
relationship, you and the other person can be
a true home for each other. In Vietnamese,
the nickname for a person's life partner is "my
home." So, for example, if a man is asked,
"Where is your wife?" he might say, "My home
is now at the post office." If a guest said to
the woman, "That meal was delicious; who
cooked it?" she might answer, "My home
prepared the meal," meaning "My husband
cooked the dinner."

OPENING THE DOOR

Once you know how to come home to yourself, then you can open your home to other people, because you have something to offer. The other person has to do exactly the same thing if they are to have something to offer you. Otherwise, they will have nothing to share but their loneliness, sickness, and suffering. This can't help heal you at all. The other person has to heal themselves and get warm inside, so that they will feel better, at ease, and can share their home with you.

HOLY INTIMACY

Sexual intimacy can be a beautiful thing if there is mindfulness, concentration, insight, mutual understanding, and love. Otherwise it will be very destructive. When the emotional, spiritual, and physical are in harmony, then intimacy can be very holy. It is easier to practice mindful intimacy as a monk than to practice as a layperson, because it's easier to refrain from sexual activity altogether than to maintain a harmonious sexual relationship. Physical intimacy should take place only when there is mutual understanding and love.

CHANNELING SEXUAL ENERGY

The Buddha was thirty-five, still very young, when he became enlightened. At this age we have a lot of sexual energy. It's wonderful if we can use this energy for the benefit of all beings, just as the Buddha did. The young monastics in our practice center spend a lot of time chopping wood, gardening, cooking, doing sitting meditation, and practicing walking meditation. They organize retreats, take care of their brothers and sisters, and of the friends who come from far away to spend time at our center and practice with us. They are using their energy in physical ways and living a fulfilling life. This helps them notice and be aware, without judgment, of sexual energy and learn to handle it well.

A STRONG ASPIRATION

If you have a deep aspiration, a goal for your life, then your loving of others is part of this aspiration and not a distraction from it. If you and your partner both want to do things to relieve the suffering in this world, then your love for each other is connected to your love for others, and it expands exponentially to cover the whole world.

WHAT LOVE NEEDS TO SURVIVE

The Buddha said that nothing survives without food, including love. If you don't know how to nourish and feed your love, it will die. If we know how to feed our love every day it will stay for a long time. One way we nourish our love is by being conscious of what we consume. Many of us think of our daily nourishment only in terms of what we eat. But in fact, there are four kinds of food that we consume every day. They are: edible food (what we put in our mouths to nourish our bodies), sensory food (what we smell, hear, taste, feel, and touch), volition (the motivation and intention that fuels us), and consciousness (this includes our individual consciousness, the collective consciousness, and our environment).

NOURISHING OUR LOVE
WITH EDIBLE FOOD

The first source of nourishment is edible food.
If we eat with moderation, eating only the food
we need and eating the foods that help our
bodies to be strong and healthy, then we're
showing love and respect for our bodies and
for the Earth. If we don't eat healthy foods and
don't treat our own bodies with respect, then
how can we respect other people's bodies
and the body of the Earth itself?

SENSORY FOOD

The second source of nourishment is sensory impressions, what we consume with our eyes, ears, nose, tongue, body, and mind. When we read a magazine, we consume. When we watch a television program, we consume. Whatever we consume affects our body and mind. If we consume toxic magazine articles, movies, or video games, they will feed our craving, our anger, and our fear. If we set aside time each day to be in a peaceful environment, to walk in nature, or even just to look at a flower or the sky, then that beauty will penetrate us and feed our love and our joy.

NOURISHING YOUR
DEEPEST DESIRE

The third nutriment is volition. This is your desire, your hope, your aspiration. It's the energy that keeps you alive. You want to *be* someone. You want to *do* something with your life. If you're motivated by compassion and love, your volition will give you the energy and direction to grow and become even more loving and compassionate. However, if your desire is to possess or to win at all costs, this kind of volition is toxic and will not help your love to grow. You can practice developing a strong and positive volition. You can even put your commitment in words, such as: "I vow to develop understanding and compassion in me, so I can become an instrument of peace and love, to help society and the world." This kind of intention is based in our deepest aspiration.

NOURISHING CONSCIOUSNESS

The fourth source of nourishment is collective
consciousness and individual consciousness.
Our individual consciousness is influenced by
the collective consciousness of our environment. We absorb and reflect what is around
us. If we live in a place where people are
angry and violent, then eventually we'll
become like them. If we live in a family or
community where there's a culture of being
understanding and compassionate with
each other, we'll naturally be more peaceful
and loving. Children growing up in such an
environment will learn to be caring and kind.

IMMEASURABLE MINDS

Loving kindness, compassion, joy, and equanimity are described as unlimited states of mind because they continue to grow and they cannot be measured. The more you practice, the more you see your love growing and growing until there is no limit. The more you practice compassion, the more it grows. The more you cultivate joy, the more joy you will feel and be able to share. The more you understand, the more you love; the more you love, the more you understand. They are two sides of one reality. The mind of love and the mind of understanding are the same.

THE BEAUTY OF THE BODY

The human body is one of the most beautiful things that we can see. We need to practice treating such beauty with reverence. Perhaps we're afraid to contemplate beauty and that's why we don't treat our bodies and the bodies of others with respect.

LONELINESS AND SEX

Sometimes we think that if we have sexual relations with someone, we'll feel less alone. But the truth is that sexual relations don't relieve loneliness. There's a Vietnamese poem in which the young man has the impression that he must sit very close to his beloved to relieve his loneliness. We have the impression that if we sit close to each other we'll feel less alone. If we're separated by five meters, that's too far. Four meters is better. Three meters is still better. But even one millimeter is still too far. When our bodies are very close, we feel it will relieve this loneliness. But if we don't share our aspirations and what's in our hearts, then even if we live together or have children together, we can still feel very alone.

DEEP LISTENING IN A COUPLE

When I meet a couple who live together and
are happy, I propose that they set up a regularly structured time of deep listening to help
them stay happy together. Deep listening is,
most of all, the practice of being present for
our loved one. We have to be truly present
for the person we love. In the person we love
there is suffering that we haven't seen yet. If
we haven't yet understood that person, we
can't be their best friend; we can't be someone who is able to understand them. It's like
when an excellent musician finds someone
who understands his music; they can become
best friends. Someone who can understand
our suffering is our best friend. We listen
to each other. We are there for each other.
Otherwise, the coming together of two bodies

becomes routine and monotonous after a time.
If you have the impression that you know the
other person inside and out, you are wrong.
Are you sure that you even know yourself?
Every person is a world to explore.

FULFILLMENT

We should practice in such a way that
every moment is fulfilling. We should feel
satisfaction in every breath, in every step,
in every action. This is true fulfillment.
When you breathe in and out, there is
fulfillment. When you take a step, there is
fulfillment. When you perform any action, there
is the fulfillment that comes from living deeply
in the present moment.

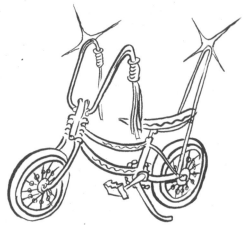

NATURAL HAPPINESS

If you walk with true awareness of every step, without having a goal to get anywhere, happiness will arise naturally. You don't need to look for happiness. When we're in touch with the wonders of life, we become aware of the many conditions of happiness that are already there, and naturally we feel happy. The beauty around us brings us back to the present moment so we can let go of the planning and worries that preoccupy us. When you look at the person you love, if he is absorbed in anxiety, you can help him get out. "Darling, do you see the sun? Do you see the signs that spring is coming?" This is mindfulness; we become aware of what is happening now and we are in touch with the conditions of happiness that are there inside us and all around us.

MEDITATION

Meditation consists of generating three kinds
of energy: mindfulness, concentration, and
insight. These three energies give us the
power to nourish happiness and take care
of our suffering. Suffering may be there. But
with the energy of mindfulness, concentration,
and insight, we can embrace and take care
of that suffering and nourish happiness at the
same time.

THE ART OF OFFERING HAPPINESS

In a friendship, we try to to offer our friend happiness. Sometimes you think that you're doing something for someone else's happiness, when actually your action is making them suffer. The willingness to make someone happy isn't enough. You have your own idea of happiness. But to make someone else happy, you have to understand that person's needs, suffering, and desires and not assume you know what will make them happy. Ask, "What would make you happy?"

THE RIGHT GIFT

In Vietnam there is a fruit that many people love called durian. It has a strong smell and it's quite expensive. Many people like it very much, but I don't like it at all. Someone who sees me working very hard might think, "Oh, Thay must be very tired; I should offer him some durian." But if you forced me to eat it, I would suffer a lot. So to love someone, you have to understand the real needs of that person, and not impose on her what you think is needed for her to be happy. Understanding is the foundation of love.

FLOWER WATERING

When we practice the art of mindful living, we water the positive elements in ourselves and each other. We see that the other person, like us, has both flowers and garbage inside, and we accept this. Our practice is to water the flower in our loved one, and not bring them more garbage. When we try to grow flowers, if they don't grow well, we don't blame them or argue with them. Our partner is a flower. If we take care of her well, she will grow beautifully. If we take care of her poorly, she will wither. To help a flower grow well, we must understand her nature. How much water and sunshine does she need?

NO SELF

Often, when we say, "I love you" we focus mostly on the idea of the "I" who is doing the loving and less on the quality of the love that's being offered. This is because we are caught by the idea of self. We think we have a self. But there is no such thing as an individual separate self. A flower is made only of non-flower elements, such as chlorophyll, sunlight, and water. If we were to remove all the non-flower elements from the flower, there would be no flower left. A flower cannot be by herself alone. A flower can only inter-be with all of us. It's much closer to the truth. Humans are like this too. We can't exist by ourselves alone. We can only inter-be. I am made only of non-me elements, such as the Earth, the sun, parents, and ancestors. In a relationship, if you can see the nature of interbeing between you and the other person, you can see that his suffering is your own suffering, and your happiness is his own happiness. With this way of seeing, you speak and act differently. This in itself can relieve so much suffering.

LOVE AS AN OFFERING

To love is not to possess the other person or to consume all their attention and love. To love is to offer the other person joy and a balm for their suffering. This capacity is what we have to learn to cultivate.

THE GREATEST GIFT

One of the greatest gifts we can offer people
is to embody nonattachment and nonfear.
This is a true teaching, more precious than
money or material resources. Many of us are
very afraid, and this fear distorts our lives and
makes us unhappy. We cling to objects and to
people like a drowning person clings to a floating log. Practicing to realize nondiscrimination,
to see the interconnectedness and impermanence of all things, and to share this wisdom
with others, we are giving the gift of nonfear.
Everything is impermanent. This moment
passes. That person walks away. Happiness is
still possible.

SHINING THE LIGHT

When we love someone, we should look deeply into the nature of that love. If we want to be with someone so that we can feel safe, that's understandable, but it's not true love. True love doesn't foster suffering or attach- ment. On the contrary, it brings well-being to ourselves and to others. True love is gener- ated from within. For true love to be there, you need to feel complete in yourself, not needing something from outside. True love is like the sun, shining with its own light, and offering that light to everyone.

LETTING GO OF NOTIONS

The notions and ideas we have about happiness can entrap us. We forget that they are just notions and ideas. Our idea of happiness may be the very thing that's preventing us from being happy. When we're caught in a belief that happiness should take a particular form, we fail to see the opportunities for joy that are right in front of us.

NO SAINTS

Don't say, "Love, compassion, joy, and equanimity are the way that saints love, so since I'm not a saint, I can't possibly love that way." The Buddha was a human being, and he practiced as we do. At first, love can be tainted with attachment, possessiveness, and the desire to control. But with the practice of mindfulness, concentration, and insight, we can transform these hindrances and have a love that is spacious, all-encompassing, and marvelous.

FRIENDSHIP

Be a friend to yourself. If you are a true friend
to yourself, you can be a true friend to a loved
one. A romantic crush is short-lived, but friendship and loving kindness can last very long
and continue to grow.

LOOKING IN THE SAME DIRECTION

Antoine de Saint-Exupéry, the author of
The Little Prince wrote that, "Love does not
consist in gazing at each other but in looking
outward in the same direction." But when two
people suffer and look in the same direction,
it is often the direction of the television! Over
time, looking at each other and speaking
with each other has become difficult and no
longer brings joy. Disagreements have gone
unresolved and tension and unhappiness have
continued to grow. How can we bring love and
happiness back into the relationship? First, we
need to reflect on how we have contributed
to this situation. Then we need to have the
courage to turn off the television and take time
to speak and listen to each other. As a true
lover, the direction you look in is peace.

A LASTING COMMITMENT

Without the pressure of other elements, what you are now calling love may turn sour very soon. The support of friends and family weaves a kind of web that helps keep a relationship strong and long-lasting. The strength of your feelings is only one strand of that web. Supported by many elements, your relationship will be solid, like a tree. To be strong, a tree sends a number of roots deep into the soil. If a tree has only one root, it may be blown over by the wind.

THE ART OF CREATING HAPPINESS

What is the nature of joy and happiness? How can we touch true joy in every moment of our lives? How can we live in a way that brings a smile, the eyes of love, and happiness to everyone we encounter? Use your talent to find ways to bring happiness to yourself and others—the happiness that arises from meditation is not the same as the feeling that comes from the pursuit of pleasure seeking. Meditative joy has the capacity to nourish our mindfulness, understanding, and love. Live in a way that encourages deep happiness in yourself and others. You can vow to bring joy to one person in the morning and to help relieve the suffering of one person in the afternoon. Ask yourself, "Who can I make smile this morning?" This is the art of creating happiness.

A SLEEPING CHILD

There are times you may sit and look at a child
when she's sleeping. While the child sleeps,
she reveals tenderness, suffering, and hope.
Just contemplate a child sleeping and observe
your feelings. Understanding and compassion
will arise in you, and you will know how to take
care of that child and make her happy. The
same is true for your partner. You should have
a chance to observe him when he sleeps.
Look deeply, and see the tenderness that
is revealed, the suffering, the hope, and the
despair that can be expressed during sleep.
Sit there for fifteen minutes or half an hour and
just look. Understanding and compassion will
arise in you, and you will know how to be there
for your partner.

LEARNING LOVE

If our parents didn't love and understand each other, how are we to know what love looks like? There aren't courses or classes in love. If the grown-ups know how to take care of each other, then the children who grow up in this environment will naturally know how to love, understand, and bring happiness to others. The most precious inheritance that parents can give their children is their own happiness. Our parents may be able to leave us money, houses, and land, but they may not be happy people. If we have happy parents, we have received the richest inheritance of all.

FORGIVENESS

Many of us wait until it is too late to see what really matters to us. Sensual desire can feel so overwhelming that it's often not until later that we see the many important things that have needed our attention. Everybody makes mistakes, but you can't keep asking people to forgive you again and again. For example, instead of just saying, "I'm sorry I shouted at you," you can train yourself not to shout so often. Instead of a quick apology, take the time and make the commitment to practice seeing the roots of your behavior.

20 QUESTIONS FOR LOOKING INTO YOUR RELATIONSHIP

1 Are you in love?

2 Are you still in love?

3 Do you want to reconnect with the person who used to be the one you love?

4 Do you think that this person is happy?

5 Do you have the time for each other?

6 Have you been able to preserve your true presence for yourself and for the other person?

7 Are you capable of offering him or her freshness every day?

8 Do you know how to handle the suffering in yourself?

9 Are you able to help handle the suffering in the other person?

10 Do you understand the roots of your own suffering?

11 Are you able to understand the suffering in the other person?

12 Do you have the capacity to help the other person suffer less?

13 Have you learned the way to calm down your painful feelings and emotions?

14 Do you have the time to listen to yourself and your deepest desire?

15 Do you have the time to listen to him or her and to help him or her suffer less?

16 Are you capable of creating a feeling of joy for yourself?

17 Are you capable of helping the other person to create a feeling of joy?

18 Do you feel you have a clear spiritual path?

19 Do you have the feeling of peace and contentment within yourself?

20 Do you know how to nourish your love every day?

PRACTICES FOR NOURISHING TRUE LOVE

THE SIX MANTRAS

ONE: I AM HERE FOR YOU

The greatest gift we can make to others is our true presence. "I am here for you" is the first of the Six Mantras. When you are concentrated, mind and body together, you produce your true presence, and anything you say is a mantra, a sacred phrase that can transform the situation. It doesn't have to be in Sanskrit or Tibetan; a mantra can be spoken in your own language. "Darling, I am here for you." If you are truly present, this mantra will produce a miracle. You become real, the other person becomes real, and life is real in that moment. You bring happiness to yourself and to the other person.

TWO: I KNOW YOU ARE THERE, AND I AM HAPPY

"I know you are there, and I am very happy" is the second of the Six Mantras. When I look at the full moon, I breathe in and out deeply and say, "Full moon, I know you are there, and I am very happy." I do the same with the morning star. When you contemplate a beautiful sunset, if you are really there, you will recognize and appreciate it deeply. Whenever you are truly there, you can recognize and appreciate the presence of the other, whether that is the full moon, the North Star, the magnolia flowers, or the person you love.

THREE: I KNOW YOU ARE SUFFERING

The third mantra is: "I know you are suffering. That is why I am here for you." When you are mindful, you will notice when the person you love suffers. If we suffer and if the person we love is not aware of our suffering, we will suffer even more. Just practice conscious breathing to produce your true presence. Then sit close to the one you love and say, "Darling, I know you suffer. That is why I am here for you." Your presence, in itself, will already relieve some of her suffering. No matter how old or young you are, you can do this.

FOUR: I AM SUFFERING

The fourth mantra is the one you can practice when you yourself suffer: "Darling, I am suffering. Please help." There are only six words, but sometimes they can be difficult to say because of the pride in our hearts, especially if we believe that it was the person we love who caused our suffering. If it had been someone else, it wouldn't be so difficult. But because it was him, we feel deeply hurt. We want to go to our room and weep. But if we really love him, when we suffer like that, we have to ask for help. We must overcome our pride.

FIVE: THIS IS A HAPPY MOMENT

The fifth mantra is, "This is a happy moment." When you're with the one you love, you can pronounce this mantra. It's not autosuggestion or wishful thinking; it's waking up to the conditions of happiness that are there. Maybe you're not mindful enough, so you don't recognize them. This mantra is to remind us that we're very lucky; we have so many conditions of happiness, and if we don't enjoy them, we're not wise at all. So when you're sitting together, walking together, eating, or doing something together, breathe in mindfully and realize how lucky you are. Mindfulness makes the present moment into a wonderful moment.

SIX: YOU ARE PARTLY RIGHT

The sixth mantra is, "You are partly right." When someone congratulates you or criticizes you, you can use this mantra. I have weakness in me and I also have strengths. If you congratulate me, I shouldn't get lost and ignore that there are negative things in me. When we see the beautiful things in the other person, we tend to ignore the things that are not so beautiful. We are human, so we have both positive and negative things in us. So when your beloved one congratulates you, and tells you that you are the very image of perfection, you say, "You are partly right. You know that I have the other things in me also." In this way, you can retain your humility. You are not a victim of illusion because you know that you're not perfect. And when another person criticizes you, you can also say, "You are partly right."

LOVE MEDITATION

This love meditation, called Metta Meditation, is adapted from the *Visuddimagga (The Path of Purification)* by Buddhaghosa, a fifth-century C.E. systematization of the Buddha's teachings.

> May I be peaceful, happy, and light in body and spirit.
> May I be safe and free from injury.
> May I be free from anger, afflictions, fear, and anxiety.

> May I learn to look at myself with the eyes of understanding and love.
> May I be able to recognize and touch the seeds of joy and happiness in myself.
> May I learn to identify and see the sources of anger, craving, and delusion in myself.

May I know how to nourish the seeds of joy
in myself every day.
May I be able to live fresh, solid, and free.
May I be free from attachment and aversion,
but not be indifferent.

To begin, sit still and calm your body and your
breathing. Sitting still, you aren't too preoccupied with other matters.

Begin practicing this love meditation on
yourself ("May I be peaceful . . ."). Until you
are able to love and take care of yourself, you
can't be of much help to others. After that,
practice on others ("May he/she/you/they be
peaceful . . .")—first on someone you like, then
on someone neutral to you, then on someone
you love, and finally on someone the mere
thought of whom makes you suffer. After practicing Metta Meditation, you may find you can
think of them with genuine compassion.

COMPASSIONATE LISTENING

In the practice of compassionate listening, you listen with only one purpose: to give the other person a chance to speak out and suffer less. Practice breathing in and out deeply and concentrate on what you are hearing. While the other person speaks, they may express bitterness, wrong perceptions, or make accusations. If you allow these things to touch off the anger in you, then you lose your capacity to listen deeply. Listening with mindfulness helps you to keep your compassion alive. It protects you, and your anger will not be triggered. Even fifteen minutes of listening like this can be very healing and can bring a lot of relief to another. You may be the first person who has ever listened to him or her like that.

SELECTIVE WATERING

Selective watering is the process of watering the good seeds and giving the healthy and positive elements in our consciousness a chance to manifest. We can organize our life in such a way that the good seeds can be touched and watered several times a day.

We are the gardeners who identify, water, and cultivate the best seeds in ourselves and in others. We need some faith that there are good seeds within us, and then, with appropriate attention, we need to touch those seeds when we practice sitting meditation, walking meditation, and throughout the day. When we succeed in touching our positive seeds once, we will know how to touch them again and again, and they will strengthen.

HUGGING MEDITATION

When we hug, our hearts connect and we know that we are not separate beings. Hugging with mindfulness and concentration can bring reconciliation, healing, understanding, and much happiness. The practice of mindful hugging has helped so many people to reconcile with each other—fathers and sons, mothers and daughters, friends and friends, and so many others.

You may practice hugging meditation with a friend, your daughter, your father, your partner, or even with a tree. Hugging is a deep practice; you need to be totally present to do it correctly. When I drink a glass of water, I invest one hundred percent of myself in drinking it. You can train yourself to live every moment of your daily life like that.

Before hugging, stand facing each other as you follow your breathing and establish your true presence. Then open your arms and hug your loved one. During the first in-breath and out-breath, become aware that you and your beloved are both alive; with the second in-breath and out-breath, think of where you will both be three hundred years from now; and with the third in-breath and out-breath, be aware of how precious it is that you are both still alive.

When you hug this way, the other person becomes real and alive. You don't need to wait until one of you is ready to depart for a trip; you may hug right now and receive the warmth and stability of your friend in the present moment. Architects need to build airports and railway stations so that there is enough room to practice hugging. When you hug in this way, your hugging will be deeper, and so will your happiness.

THE FIVE AWARENESSES

These verses can be practiced by anyone at anytime to help safeguard our relationships. Many people have used them in weddings and commitment ceremonies, and some couples like to say them to each other weekly. If you have a bell, you can invite it to sound after you recite each verse. Then breathe in and out a few times in silence before going on to the next verse.

1. We are aware that all generations of our ancestors and all future generations are present in us.
2. We are aware of the expectations that our ancestors, our children, and their children have of us.

3. We are aware that our joy, peace, freedom, and harmony are the joy, peace, freedom, and harmony of our ancestors, our children, and their children.

4. We are aware that understanding is the very foundation of love.

5. We are aware that blaming and arguing can never help us and only create a wider gap between us; that only understanding, trust, and love can help us change and grow.

RELATED TITLES

Awakening Joy by James Baraz and
Shoshana Alexander

Beginning Anew by Sister Chan Khong

Being Peace by Thich Nhat Hanh

Happiness by Thich Nhat Hanh

How to Eat by Thich Nhat Hanh

How to Sit by Thich Nhat Hanh

How to Walk by Thich Nhat Hanh

Teachings on Love by Thich Nhat Hanh

Ten Breaths to Happiness by Glen Schneider

Monastics and visitors practice the art of mindful living in the tradition of Thich Nhat Hanh at our ten mindfulness practice centers around the world. For a full listing of practice centers, or for information about retreats, visit plumvillage.org or contact:

Plum Village
33580 Dieulivol, France
plumvillage.org

Deer Park Monastery
Escondido, CA 92026, USA
deerparkmonastery.org

Magnolia Grove Monastery
Batesville, MS 38606, USA
magnoliagrovemonastery.org

Blue Cliff Monastery
Pine Bush, NY 12566, USA
bluecliffmonastery.org

European Institute of
Applied Buddhism
D-51545 Waldbröl, Germany
eiab.eu

Thailand Plum Village
Nakhon Ratchasima,
30130 Thailand
phfhk.org

The Mindfulness Bell, a journal of the art of mindful living in the tradition of Thich Nhat Hanh, is published three times a year by our community. To subscribe or to see the worldwide directory of Sanghas, or local mindfulness groups, visit mindfulnessbell.org.

The Thich Nhat Hanh Foundation supports Thich Nhat Hanh's peace work and mindfulness teachings around the world. For more information on how you can help or on how to nourish your mindfulness practice, visit the foundation at tnhf.org.

**PARALLAX
PRESS**

Parallax Press, a nonprofit publisher founded by
Zen Master Thich Nhat Hanh, publishes books
and media on the art of mindful living and
Engaged Buddhism. We are committed to offering
teachings that help transform suffering and
injustice. Our aspiration is to contribute to collective
insight and awakening, bringing about a more
joyful, healthy, and compassionate society.

View our entire library at **parallax.org**.

HOW TO
SIT

THICH NHAT HANH

PARALLAX
PRESS

BERKELEY, CALIFORNIA

Parallax Press
P.O. Box 7355
Berkeley, California 94707

Parallax Press is the publishing division of Plum
Village Community of Engaged Buddhism, Inc.
Copyright © 2014 Plum Village Community
of Engaged Buddhism, Inc.
Printed in Canada

Cover and text design by Debbie Berne
Illustrations by Jason DeAntonis
Edited by Rachel Neumann

ISBN: 978-1-937006-58-7

Library of Congress Cataloging-in-Publication Data
Nhat Hanh, Thich, author.
How to sit / Thich Nhat Hanh.
    pages cm
Includes bibliographical references.
ISBN 978-1-937006-58-7
1. Meditation—Buddhism. I. Title.
BQ5612.N474 2014
294.3'4435—dc23
                                    2014000019

9 10 / 22

CONTENTS

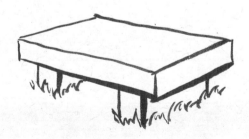

The first thing to do is to stop
whatever else you are doing.

Now sit down somewhere comfortable.

Anywhere is fine.

Notice your breathing.

As you breathe in,
be aware
that you are
breathing in.

As you breathe out,
notice that you are
breathing out.

NOTES ON SITTING

Many of us spend a lot of time sitting—too much time. We sit at our jobs, we sit at our computers, and we sit in our cars. To *sit*, in this book, means to sit in such a way that you enjoy sitting, to sit in a relaxed way, with your mind awake, calm, and clear. This is what we call *sitting*, and it takes some training and practice.

BODY, MIND, AND BREATH

In our daily lives, our attention is dispersed. Our body is in one place, our breath is ignored, and our mind is wandering. As soon as we pay attention to our breath, as we breathe in, these three things—body, breath, and mind—come together. This can happen in just one or two seconds. You come back to yourself. Your awareness brings these three elements together, and you become fully present in the here and the now. You are taking care of your body, you are taking care of your breath, and you are taking care of your mind.

When you make a soup, you have to add together all the right ingredients in harmony and let them simmer. Our breath is the broth that brings the different elements together. We bathe spirit and mind in our breath and they become integrated so they are one thing. We are whole.

We don't need to control our body, mind, and breath. We can just be there for them. We allow them to be themselves. This is nonviolence.

PEACE IS CONTAGIOUS

The energy of mindfulness can help improve your whole being. Just pay attention to your in-breath. Allow it to be the way it is and you will see that the quality of your breathing naturally becomes calmer, deeper, and more harmonious all by itself. This is the power of simple recognition. When your breath is deeper and more peaceful, it will have an influence right away on your body and your mind. Peace and calm are contagious.

A BOAT ON THE OCEAN

Imagine a boat full of people crossing the ocean. The boat is caught in a storm. If anyone panics and acts rashly they will endanger the boat. But if there's even one person who is calm, this person can inspire calm in others. Such a person can save the whole boat. That's the power of non-action. Our quality of being is the ground of all appropriate action. When we look closely at our actions and the actions of those around us, we can see the quality of being behind these actions.

DOING NOTHING

Imagine trees standing together in a forest. They don't talk, but they feel each other's presence. When you look at them, you might say they aren't doing anything. But they are growing and providing clean air for living things to breathe. Instead of describing sitting meditation as the practice of concentration, looking deeply, and getting insight, I like to describe sitting as enjoying doing nothing. Primarily, sitting is to enjoy the pleasure of sitting, being fully alive and in touch with the wonders of our working bodies, the cool air, the sounds of people and birds, and the changing colors of the sky.

MEDITATION

The term for sitting and being aware is sitting meditation. "Zen" is the Japanese pronunciation of *dhyana*, which is the Sanskrit word for meditation. Meditation is simply the practice of stopping and looking deeply. You do not need to sit to meditate. Anytime you are looking deeply—whether you are walking, chopping vegetables, brushing your teeth, or going to the bathroom—you can be meditating. In order to look deeply, you need to make the time to stop everything and see what is there.

With mindfulness and concentration you can direct your attention to what is there and have a deep look. You can begin to see the true nature of what is in front of you. What is there may be a cloud, a pebble, or a human being. It may be our anger. Or it may be our own body and its nature of impermanence. Every time we truly stop and look deeply, the result is a better understanding of the true nature of what is there inside us and around us.

DON'T JUST DO SOMETHING, SIT THERE

When people say, "Don't just sit there, do something," they're urging you to act. But if the quality of your being is poor—if you don't have enough peace, understanding, and equanimity, if you still have a lot of anger and worries—then your actions will also be poor. Your actions should be based on the foundation of a high quality of being. Being is non-action, so the quality of action depends on the quality of non-action. Non-action is already something. There are people who don't seem to do very much, but their presence is crucial for the well-being of the world. You may know people like this, who are steady, not always busy doing things, not making a lot of money, or being engaged in a lot of projects, but who are very important to you; the quality of their presence makes them truly available. They are contributing non-action, the high quality of their presence. To be in the here and the now—solid and fully alive—is a very positive contribution to our collective situation.

THE MONK ON THE PLATFORM

When I was a novice monk in Vietnam, I went to a temple called Hai Duc where I saw a Zen master sitting. He wasn't in the meditation hall. He was sitting on a simple platform made from perhaps five planks of wood. It was painted brown and was very clean. On the platform was a small table with four legs that were a little bit bent. That little table had a vase of flowers on it. I saw the Zen master sitting on the platform, facing the table. He was sitting very naturally and peacefully, his spine straight and his body at ease.

As a young child, I saw a drawing of the Buddha sitting on the grass. He looked very free, relaxed, and peaceful, as well as very kind. Now I was seeing a real human being sitting like that. This was a person like me, not an illustration or someone belonging to another world. Seeing the monk on the platform was a very holy experience. I wanted to be able to sit like that monk. I knew that sitting like that would bring me happiness.

DOING LESS

Many of us keep trying to do more and more. We do things because we think we need to, because we want to make money, accomplish something, take care of others, or make our lives and our world better. Often we do things without thinking, because we are in the habit of doing them, because someone asks us to, or because we think we should. But if the foundation of our being is not strong enough, then the more we do, the more troubled our society becomes.

Sometimes we do a lot, but we don't really do anything. There are many people who work a lot. There are people who seem to meditate a lot, spending many hours a day doing sitting meditation, chanting, reciting, lighting a lot of incense, but who never transform their anger, frustration, and jealousy. This is because the quality of our being is the basis of all our actions. With an attitude of accomplishing, judging, or grasping, all of our actions—even our meditation—will have that quality. The quality of our presence is the most positive element that we can contribute to the world.

ENJOY YOUR BREATHING

When you sit down, the first thing to do is to become aware of your breathing. Becoming aware of your breathing is the first step in taking care of yourself. Becoming aware of your in-breath and out-breath, you can see how your breath moves through your body. You begin to take care of your body and your mind, and you begin to find joy in the very simple act of breathing. Every in-breath can bring joy; every out-breath can bring calm and relaxation. This is a good enough reason to sit. We don't need to sit with an intention like getting smarter or becoming enlightened. We can sit just to enjoy sitting and breathing.

THE JOY OF MEDITATION

If you ask a child, "Why are you eating choco-late? The child would likely answer, "Because I like it." There's no purpose in eating the choc-olate. Suppose you climb a hill and stand on top to look around. You might feel quite happy standing on the hill. There's not a reason for doing it. Sit in order to sit. Stand in order to stand. There is no goal or aim in sitting. Do it because it makes you happy.

A CELEBRATION

If you are breathing mindfully in and out, you already have insight. Everyone is breathing, but not everyone is aware that they're breathing. When you breathe in mindfully, you realize that you are alive. If you weren't alive, you wouldn't be breathing in. To be alive is the greatest of all miracles, and you can rejoice in being alive. When you breathe in this way, your breath is a celebration of life.

FOLLOWING OUR BREATH

Mindfulness is always mindfulness of *something*. When we are mindful, we are paying attention, but what are we paying attention to? Mindfulness always has an object. When we sit, we can become aware of our in-breath and out-breath. Follow your breath from the beginning of each inhale all the way through the end of each exhale. This is mindfulness of breathing. Each time we practice mindful breathing, we know a little more what mindfulness feels like.

LOOKING DEEPLY

Sitting meditation is a practice that helps us heal and transform. It helps us to be whole, and to look deeply into ourselves and into what's around us in order to see clearly what is really there. Looking deeply, we light up the recesses of our mind and look into the heart of things in order to see their true nature.

MEDITATION IN DAILY LIFE

When most people hear the word "meditation," they think of sitting meditation. There are many different kinds of meditation. Mindfulness meditation can be practiced anywhere and in whatever position the body is in—whether we are sitting, walking, standing, or lying down. Whenever we perform our daily activities with mindful awareness, we're practicing meditation.

WISDOM

By looking deeply, the meditation practitioner gains insight or wisdom, *prajña*. Insight has the power to liberate us from our own suffering and bondage. In the process of meditation, fetters are undone; internal blocks of suffering such as resentment, fear, anger, despair, and hatred are transformed; relationships with humans and nature become easier; freedom and joy can penetrate us. We become aware of what is inside and around us; we are fresher and more alive in our daily lives. As we become freer and happier, we cease to act in ways that make others suffer, and we are able to bring about change in ourselves and help others around us become free.

WHY SIT?

When we sit, we bring joy and nourishment to
ourselves and to others. Every time we sit, we
can sit in such a way that the world can profit
from our sitting. We are solid. We are relaxed.
We are calm. We are happy while sitting. We
sit as if we are sitting on a lotus flower, not on
a heap of burning charcoal.

THE MOMENT OF ENLIGHTENMENT

Siddhartha, the man who became the Buddha many years ago in India, sat for a long time at the foot of the Bodhi tree. He appeared just to be sitting, but his body was also participating in his awakening. He was very closely observing his body, his feelings, and his perceptions. As he continued to practice, his power of mindfulness and concentration became stronger and stronger. One day at dawn, as the Morning Star appeared, he felt a liberation that dissipated all the darkness within him. That was the moment of enlightenment.

THE NON-PRACTICE PRACTICE

There are some people who sit in a very funny way; they try to show that they are practicing sitting meditation. When you breathe in mindfully and joyfully, don't try to show off to other people as if you were saying, "You know, I am breathing in mindfully." Don't worry what your sitting looks like from the outside. Practice the non-practice practice. We can best convey the essence of the practice to others simply by doing it with our whole being.

ARRIVING HOME

When you sit, sit in such a way that you feel
you have already arrived. To sit doesn't mean
to struggle. When you sit, sit so that sitting
becomes an arrival into the present moment.
Enjoy your arrival. How wonderful to have
arrived. How wonderful to feel that you are
home, that your true home is in the here
and the now. Sitting like that, joy and peace
become a reality. You radiate this joy and
peace and it benefits everyone around you.

FREEDOM

In the present moment, we can be free from regret concerning the past and from fear concerning the future. Happiness isn't possible without freedom. Coming back to the present moment, we are released from our worries, our fears, our regrets, our projects, and our busyness.

NOURISH YOURSELF
WHEREVER YOU ARE

It's wonderful if you have a quiet place to sit at home or in your workplace. But you can practice mindful sitting wherever you are. If you ride the train or the bus to work, these are excellent places to practice sitting. Instead of thinking about your projects, your colleagues, your list of tasks, you can enjoy practicing breathing in and out to release the tension in your body and give your mind a break from being caught in thinking. You can create a meditation hall of your bus or your train. Use your time, wherever you are, to nourish and heal yourself.

SITTING COMFORTABLY

When you sit, keep your spinal column quite straight, while allowing your body to be relaxed. When your sitting posture is relaxed and stable, you can sit comfortably for a long time. You embody solidity and this helps your mind to be calm. A stable posture grounds body and mind. Sitting still, we minimize the actions of body, speech, and mind so we're not pulled hither and thither by thoughts and feelings in which we might otherwise drown.

UNDER THE BODHI TREE

A gatha is a traditional short verse that you
can recite during your meditation. You can
make your own, or recite ones you have heard.
Here is one:

Sitting here
is like sitting under the bodhi tree.
My body is mindfulness itself,
entirely free from distraction.

SITTING IN PRISON

A Vietnamese student of mine studied English literature at Indiana University before return-ing to Vietnam and being ordained as a nun. As a nun, she was very active in trying to ease the suffering of people's daily lives. She was arrested by the police and put into prison because of her actions. She would practice sitting meditation in her prison cell. It was dif-ficult, because the guards saw her sitting as a provocative action. They thought she was defying them by sitting peacefully. She would wait until night, when all the lights were off, so she could sit like a free person. The people who put her in prison were trying to control her. She had to practice so she wouldn't lose her mind; sitting like that gave her space in her heart. She also taught others who were incarcerated how to sit and breathe so that they would suffer less. In her outer form, she was caught in prison. Yet she was completely free. If you can sit like that, the walls are not there. You are in touch with the whole universe. You have more freedom than people outside who are imprisoning themselves with their agitation and anger. People can try to steal many things from us, but they can't steal our determination and our practice.

EASE

Sit in such a way that you feel completely at ease. Relax every muscle in your body, including the muscles in your face. The best way to relax the muscles in your face is to smile gently as you breathe in and out. Don't make a great effort, or struggle, or fight as you sit. Let go of everything. This prevents backache, shoulderache, or headache. If you are able to find a cushion that fits your body well, you can sit for a long time without feeling tired.

WHAT TO DO

Sometimes people say they don't know what to do when they are sitting. "You only need to sit" is an exhortation of the Soto Zen meditation school. It means that you should sit without waiting for a miracle, and that includes the miracle of enlightenment. If you always sit in expectation, you're not in the present moment. The present moment contains the whole of life.

LETTING GO

Sit in such a way that you feel light, relaxed, happy, and free. Many of us have so many anxieties and projects that weigh heavily on us. We carry our past sorrows and anger and they become a kind of baggage that makes life heavy. Sitting meditation is a way to practice letting go of the things we carry needlessly. These things are nothing but obstacles to our happiness. Ease in our sitting and ease in our breathing nourishes the body and mind.

When we are calm, we can look deeply into a difficult emotion to see its roots and

understand it better. First, we nourish ourselves with the joy of meditation, calming the
breath, body, and thoughts. Then we embrace
the difficult feeling. This brings some relief and
gives us a more solid basis for investigating
and transforming the difficulty so we can get
the healing we need.

Finally, we can explore if our emotion is
based on something happening in the present
or something that we are still attached to from
the past. If it's from the past we can begin to
let it go, to more truly see and experience the
present moment.

SMILING

As you sit, consider smiling lightly. This should be a natural smile, not a grimace or a forced smile. Your smile relaxes all your facial muscles. When you smile to your whole body, it is as if you are bathed in a fresh, cool stream of water.

HAPPINESS

Relaxing and calming the body as we breathe in and out, we can already experience joy and happiness. This is the joy of being alive, of being able to nourish the body at the same time as the soul. To sit knowing that we don't have to do anything but breathe in and out in awareness is a great happiness. Countless people bounce about like yo-yos in their busy lives and never have the chance to taste this joy. Don't worry if you don't have hours to dedicate to sitting. A few moments of sitting and conscious breathing can bring great happiness.

BREATHING ROOM

Every time you sit, whether it's at work, at the foot of a tree, or on your meditation cushion at home, enjoy your sitting. Then you won't consider sitting to be hard practice. It's very pleasant. Set aside a room or a corner or a cushion that you use just for sitting. When you arrive there, you will immediately begin to feel some of the joy and relaxation that comes from sitting. Whether sitting alone or with a few friends, you can produce your full presence, your true presence.

SITTING WITH THE BELL

The sound of the bell is a wonderful way to begin sitting meditation. The sound of the bell is the voice of your own true self, calling you back to the present moment. The beautiful sound reminds us that our true home is in the present moment. Listening to the bell supports meditation practice. Be aware of your breathing when listening to the bell.

INVITING THE BELL

Instead of "striking the bell," I like to say "inviting the bell to sound." Breathe in and out three times and then wake up the bell by touching the inviter to the bell and leaving it there, causing a muffled sound. Then breathe in and out one time before inviting a full sound of the bell. If you don't have a bell, you can download a recording of the sound of the bell onto your phone or computer.*

*http://plumvillage.org/mindfulness-practice/mindfulness-software/

LISTENING TO THE BELL

When we sit and listen to the bell, we can allow all the cells in our body to listen to the sound. The mind is also made of something like "cells." These are our thoughts, feelings, and perceptions, and our ideas about how things are and should be. All the mental formations exist in the unconscious mind as seeds. When a seed, for example the seed of anger, is touched, it manifests in the conscious mind and there we call it a mental formation. Whatever mental formation has arisen in us, we can allow it to listen to the bell. Whether it is worry, anger, fear, or attachment, we allow the mental formation to listen to the bell with us. Just as a flower is made of non-flower elements, we are made of non-us elements. We are made of ancestors, culture, food, air, and water. We are made of form, feelings, perceptions, mental formations, and consciousness. We invite every component to listen deeply to the bell. This way of listening brings peace into every cell of the body and mind.

ACCOMPANYING YOUR BREATH

If you have a bell at home, anyone can invite it at any time to bring everyone back to themselves. Every time you hear the bell, you stop everything you are saying, doing, or thinking. Ride on the sound of the bell and on your breath to go home to yourself, to go home to the present moment, to the here and the now. You learn the art of being alive, of being present. To be alive means to be in the here and the now so we can be in touch with the wonders of life within us and around us. The practice is simple. Every time you hear the bell, it's as if someone is calling you, "Come home, my child, don't run anymore. Come home to yourself. Come home to life."

CREATING A GOOD HABIT

If you sit regularly, it will become a habit. You will let go of trying to arrive anywhere. Even the Buddha still practiced sitting every day after his enlightenment. There is nowhere to arrive except the present moment.

HABIT ENERGY

When you sit, you may feel something pushing you to get up and do something else. That's the energy inside each of us called habit energy. Habit energy is energy that is fueled by an old pattern, situation, or habit. It isn't based on our real needs and our real situation in the present.

Habit energy is always pushing. We have the habit of thinking that happiness isn't possible in the here and now, that we have to go and look for it somewhere else or in the future.

That's why we keep running. Our parents ran too. They transmitted the habit of running to us, and they received it from their ancestors. It's a longstanding habit. We deeply believe that in the future we may have more conditions for our happiness and that our "real life" lies somewhere else. It's because of our habit energy, that the present moment can seem boring.

It is a strong energy. If we are not aware of it, it can be stronger than we are. When we sit and invite the sound of the bell, it is a reminder to let go of that habit energy and return home.

ON THE BUS IN INDIA

Some years ago I went to India to give retreats
for the Dalit people. They're considered the
lowest caste in Indian society, and have been
discriminated against for thousands of years.
Many of them have embraced Buddhism
because there are no castes in Buddhist practice. A Dalit man from the Buddhist Society
was helping organize our tour. He had a family,
an apartment in New Delhi, and a comfortable
material life, but he still carried the habit energies of his class and the discrimination against
him. I was sitting next to him in the bus, enjoying looking out of the window at the landscape
of India. When I turned my head back, I saw
him sitting in a very tense way. While I was
enjoying sitting in the bus, he wasn't enjoying

it at all. I said, "Dear friend, I know that you're eager to make my visit pleasant and happy. I'm feeling very comfortable and happy right now, so please sit back and relax, don't worry." He said, "Okay," and he sat back and relaxed while I looked out of the window again and enjoyed the scenery. When I looked back a few minutes later, I saw him again as rigid as before, because those worries, feelings, and that tendency always to be struggling had been handed down to him by many generations of ancestors. It's not easy just to stop and recognize old habit energies. We all need a friend to help remind us from time to time. If no one else is there, the sound of the bell can be that friend, reminding us to recognize and smile at our old habit energies. In that way, we can become free of them.

SEEING CLEARLY

The first thing to do when you sit down is to pay attention to your in-breath and out-breath. Focus your attention entirely on your breathing. If you truly practice, your breath will become peaceful. This peaceful breathing will soothe both mind and body. This is the first priority of sitting meditation, to help us calm down. Once we are calm, we can see more clearly. And when our vision is no longer clouded, we see with more understanding, and we naturally begin to feel compassion for ourselves and for others. That is when true happiness becomes possible.

GIFTS OF THE PRACTICE

Sitting and breathing mindfully brings four important elements into our lives: peace, clarity, compassion, and courage. When we are peaceful and clear, we are inspired to be more compassionate. Compassion brings courage, and courage brings true happiness. When you have great compassion in yourself, you have the capacity to act with courage. You have enough courage to look deeply at old habits, acknowledge fear, and make decisions that can cut through craving and anger. If you don't have enough compassion for yourself and for others, you won't have the courage to cut off the afflictions that make you suffer.

RECOGNIZING THE BODY

When our in-breath and out-breath become peaceful and pleasant, our bodies begin to benefit. In our daily lives, many of us forget that we have a body. Our bodies often contain stress, pain, and suffering. Often we ignore the body until the pain gets too great. If we breathe peacefully, this peace will be transmitted to the body. Sitting and breathing mindfully, we bring the mind back to the body and begin to recognize its presence and release the tension held there.

SITTING IS A PRACTICE
AND A LUXURY

Sitting is a practice. The kind of sitting we're used to doing is sitting in order to work at our computers, to be in meetings, or to space out in front of a screen. So we have to practice sitting just to be with ourselves without distractions. In our time, in our civilization, sitting and doing nothing is considered either to be a luxury or a waste of time. But sitting can produce the most nourishing calm and joy and we can all afford some time to sit. How wonderful to sit and do nothing.

WHAT IS ESSENTIAL

What is essential is to train to sit quietly and mindfully. The more you train yourself, the more you can reach the deeper aspect of what you are thinking and feeling. You might think: "I'm bored!" "This is stupid." "I need to do something else right this minute." There may be old habits and old stories that are creating those thoughts and those feelings. What is getting in the way of your being able to experience the present moment? Keep breathing. Keep sitting. This is the practice.

A RIVER OF FEELINGS

There's a river of feeling in every one of us—
pleasant feelings, unpleasant feelings, and
neutral feelings. They come one after another
like drops of water in the river. As we sit, the
river of feelings runs through us and it's tempt-
ing to let a strong feeling pull us downstream.
Instead, we sit on the riverbank and observe
the feelings as they run through us. We can
name them. "This is a pleasant feeling." "This
is a painful feeling." We can do the same with
our mental formations, such as anger and fear.
Naming can be a first step in giving us some
distance from our feelings, so we can see that
a feeling is just a feeling and that it is impermanent. A feeling comes and eventually it goes.

WEATHERING THE STORM OF STRONG EMOTIONS

A strong emotion is like a storm and it can create a lot of damage. We need to know how to protect ourselves and create a safe environment where we can weather the storm. Keeping our body and mind safe from the storm is our practice. After each storm, we will became stronger, more solid, and less fearful of the storms.

We can learn to take care of the painful feelings and strong emotions emerging from the depth of our consciousness. We are more than our emotions. We can recognize what is there, "Breathing in, I know that this is only an emotion. It's not the whole of me. I am more than my emotions." This is a very basic insight. Emotions will manifest, stay for a while, and then leave. Why should we die because of one emotion? After a few minutes of practice, the storm will die down, and you will see how easily you have survived. You should start your practice before the storm begins or you might forget to do it, and may get carried away by the storm. This is why our daily practice is important.

BELLY BREATHING

Each time a storm comes up sit quietly and return to your breathing and your body. Turn your attention away from whatever it is that you believe is the source of your suffering and instead focus on your breathing. Mindful breathing is your anchor in the storm. Bring your attention away from your head and down to your belly, so that you're no longer thinking and imagining. Just follow your breathing closely. Remind yourself, "I have passed through many storms. Every storm has to pass; no storm stays forever. This state of mind will pass."

When we see the top of a tree being tossed about in a storm, we have the feeling that the tree may be blown down at any moment. But if we look at the trunk of the tree, we see it's very steady, and we know that the tree will stand strong. Your belly is like the trunk of the tree. Practice breathing with your mind only focused on breathing into your lower belly and just let your emotions go by.

NEUTRAL FEELINGS

When you sit and breathe with mindful awareness, you become aware of all the emotions
that have been ignored while you were busy
doing things. You become aware not just of
your sorrows and joys but also of your neutral
feelings. A neutral feeling is an awareness
that is neither pleasant nor painful, such as an
awareness of a part of your body that is not in
pain. With awareness, we can transform a neutral feeling into a pleasant feeling.

When you have a toothache, the feeling is
very unpleasant. When you don't have a toothache, you usually have a neutral feeling; you're
not aware of your non-toothache. When you
are mindful of not having a toothache, then

what was a neutral feeling becomes a feeling of peace and joy. You are so happy not to have a toothache in this moment. By transforming neutral feelings into joyful ones, we nourish our happiness.

TRANSFORMING CONSCIOUSNESS

The first aspect of sitting meditation is to stop and calm the body. This in itself can be a source of great happiness. But there is a second aspect of sitting meditation that can bring even more happiness. To look deeply is to do the work of transforming the depths of your consciousness. There are people who meditate only to forget the complications and problems of life. They are like rabbits crouching under a hedge to escape a potential hunter. When we look deeply we are able to see the source of our habits, perceptions, and attachments. Looking with compassion and without judgment, we begin to let go of these perceptions and are able to see the world and ourselves more clearly.

BRINGING OUR SITTING WITH US INTO THE WORLD

If you begin to feel the security and protection that arises naturally from sitting in meditation, you may be reluctant to leave this state. But we can't continue to sit forever. We can continue our mindful awareness in every action, in how we walk, talk, and work. In this way, we engage fully in life and are able to bring joy to our relationships and our world.

THE STARS OVERHEAD

No matter where we are, whenever we're sitting, over our heads there is a river of trillions of stars. We are sitting on a planet, a very beautiful planet, which is revolving in the Milky Way galaxy. When we sit with that awareness, we can embrace the whole world, from the past to the future. When we sit like that, our happiness is very great.

BE PRESENT WHERE YOU ARE

When we have the capacity to be peaceful and joyful as we sit, we can sit anywhere. We can sit in the airport. We can sit in the train station. We can sit on the bank of a river. We can sit in prison. If everyone in the world knew how to sit like that, this world would have more peace, joy, and happiness.

When we're sitting, we're truly there in the present moment; we have come home, we have arrived. We are present in that time and place; we're not pulled away by the past, the future, or by anger or jealousy in the present. When we sit like that, we sit as a free person.

A FLOWER BETWEEN
TWO ROCKS

When you sit alone quietly, it's something
beautiful, even if nobody sees it. When a little
flower appears in a crack between two rocks,
it's a beautiful sight. People may never see it,
but that's okay.

SITTING AND MOPPING

How we sit can be applied at any moment during our daily lives. For example, when we mop the floor, we mop the floor just to mop the floor, and we enjoy mopping the floor. We are happy. The happiness and contentment we experience in sitting meditation can be brought into daily life. We can be happy mopping the floor.

RESTORING OURSELVES

In our daily lives we may get lost in our thinking, in our worries, and in our various projects. To sit is to restore ourselves, to become fully present and fully alive in the here and the now. Following your breathing, calming your body and mind, you can become present easily and quickly. It takes five or ten seconds for us to restore ourselves fully and produce our true presence in the here and the now. We offer that quality of being to ourselves, to each other, and to the world.

SPIRITUAL FOOD

Sitting isn't something we do as a duty or an obligation. Instead it can be part of our daily nourishment, like eating. Consider daily sitting meditation to be a kind of spiritual food. When we sit, we produce the energy of mindfulness and a feeling of ease that nourishes our joy. Try to practice sitting meditation regularly. Don't deprive yourself and the world of this spiritual food. When we can see that our practice is nourishment for ourselves and for the world, it brings us joy and the feeling that we're useful to life.

COUNTING THE BREATH

When we're first learning sitting meditation, it can be useful to count our breaths. Count "one" for the first in- and out-breath. Count "two" for the second, and so on. If your mind wanders and you lose count, go back to "one" and begin again. This exercise helps develop concentration. You may think counting to ten is easy, but counting to ten while breathing mindfully takes a lot of focus.

USING A CLOCK

If you have a clock that makes an audible sound, try breathing in accordance with the rhythm of the clock. This can help you stop thinking and focus instead on your breathing.

A SITTING NOTEBOOK

It can be useful to keep a notebook to jot down notes while sitting or to write in after sitting. If you sit in the same place each time, you can keep the notebook there. If you sit in different places wherever or whenever you can, then keep your notebook with you in a bag or backpack. You can write down the thoughts that come to you, the insights you have. You can also draw. Writing when your mind is clear after sitting can be very satisfying. You don't need to read it right away. Perhaps leave it for a while, so you can continue to reflect without judgment.

WE ARE A STREAM

Even when you think you are sitting alone, your ancestors are sitting with you. Your parents, grandparents, and great-grandparents, whether you knew them or not, are there inside of you. Acknowledge them and invite them to breathe with you: "Dear father, these are my lungs, and they're also your lungs. I know that you are in every cell in my body." Breathing in, you can say, "Mother, I invite you to breathe in and out with me." In every cell of your body, your ancestors are there. You can invite all your ancestors to enjoy breathing in and out with you. You are not an isolated being. You are made of ancestors. When you breathe out calmly, all your ancestors in you breathe out calmly. When they were alive, they might not have had a chance to sit mindfully and breathe peacefully. But now, in you, they have that chance. There is no separate self. We are a current. We are a stream. We are a continuation.

SITTING WITH OUR SPIRITUAL ANCESTORS

When you sit, you are sitting with your blood ancestors, but you are also sitting with your spiritual ancestors as well. Your spiritual ancestors are also part of you. You can invite those who inspire you; you can invite Moses, Jesus, or Mohammed to breathe in with you and enjoy breathing. They are also in every one of our cells.

SITTING TOGETHER

Sitting alone is wonderful. Sitting with a friend makes meditation easier. There is a Vietnamese phrase that goes like this: "When you eat rice, you need to have soup." When you practice mindfulness, you have to have friends. When we sit together, we create a collective energy of mindfulness that is very powerful. When we sit with others, we profit from their quality of being and we profit from everyone's practice. We don't need to say a lot, but we become a collective organism and together we produce insight. When we sit together, each one of us contributes to the quality of the whole. This collective energy is more powerful than our individual energy. Sitting together is like allowing the water in the stream to be embraced by the ocean. When we hear the sound of the bell, everyone is breathing mindfully amd creating a collective energy of mindfulness. The collective energy is very supportive and effective in helping us gain insight and transform difficulties. As a practitioner we can benefit from that energy to help us embrace our pain and our suffering. You can say silently, "Dear brothers and sisters in the Sangha, this is my suffering. Please brothers and sisters, please help me to embrace this pain and this suffering."

A FLOCK OF BIRDS

When you practice sitting with others, you don't have to do anything at all. The basic practice is to be there, to follow your breathing, and to experience the joy of being together. Imagine a flock of birds flying in the sky. Every bird has its own position and each bird makes a contribution to the whole formation. They fly so smoothly together. Since each bird is part of this larger formation, they don't have to make a lot of effort. They benefit from the collective energy and don't need to work as hard. It's a pleasure to fly together like that in the sky. When we sit together, we are supported by each other. We each produce our true presence and offer that to each other.

HELPING EACH OTHER

When you sit with others, you are taking
care of yourself and you are taking care of
the group. If you see someone sitting solidly
and calmly, this can help you. Such a person
affects the whole environment. When I see
someone sitting like this, I want to sit like him.
I want to offer my true presence. My presence can also have a quality that can help the
community. The collective energy penetrates
everyone. Everyone offers and everyone
receives at the same time.

HELPING A FRIEND

There may be someone sitting with you who is holding a big block of fear or despair, but who isn't saying anything. She is trying to hold it as she sits. If you are sitting there, present and solid, you are already helping her. Your presence says, "Don't worry, I am here with you. I will help you to embrace and hold that fear and despair in you." Alone, it is difficult to hold a lot of pain. But with the collective energy of the group, it becomes possible.

A GARDENER RETURNING TO THE GARDEN

When you sit, you are like a gardener going back to take care of his or her garden. All the plants and animals in the garden benefit from the gardener's return. They are so happy to have the gardener back. When you sit, you are coming back to yourself, to your body, your feelings, your emotions, and your perceptions in order to take care of them. That's good news.

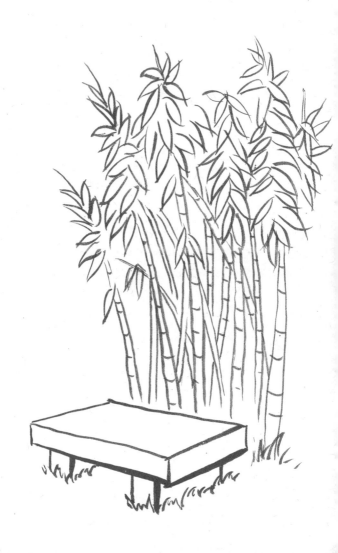

GUIDED
MEDITATIONS

Guided meditation is not a new invention.
It was used in the time of the Buddha, over
2,500 years ago. Even if you enjoy sitting in
silence, guided meditation can be beneficial.
A guided meditation is an opportunity to look
deeply into the mind, to sow wholesome
seeds there, and to strengthen and cultivate
those seeds so that they may become the
means for transforming the suffering in us. A
guided meditation can also help us come face
to face with suffering we have been avoiding.
Seeing it more clearly, we can understand its
root causes and be free of its bondage.

JOY

As you sit, you can try these meditations for bringing joy and calmness into your body. Each short verse is called a practice poem or *gatha*. The first time through, read each whole sentence to yourself. The second time through, you can just use the keywords on the third line. Silently say one word as you inhale and one word as you exhale. You can stay with those words for a few in- and out-breaths, before moving on to the next part of the exercise.

Breathing in, give complete attention to your in-breath. Wherever the breath may be in your body, feel the calm it brings. Feel how the breath cools the inner organs of the body, just like drinking cool water on a hot day. While breathing out, smile to relax all your facial muscles, and your nervous system will also relax.

These guided meditations are lights to guide us back into the present moment. They are short and can be practiced anywhere at any time: in the kitchen, on the bank of a river, in a park, whether we are walking or standing still, lying down, or sitting, even when we are working. The first meditation shows how the breath goes with the words. It works the same for all the following meditations.

1 Breathing in, I know I am
   breathing in. *(inhale)*
   Breathing out, I know I am
   breathing out. *(exhale)*
   In *(inhale)* / Out *(exhale)*

2 Breathing in, my breath grows deep.

   Breathing out, my breath goes slowly.

   Deep / Slow

3 Breathing in, I feel calm.

   Breathing out, I feel ease.

   Calm / Ease

4 Breathing in, I smile.

   Breathing out, I release.

   Smile / Release

5 Aware of my body, I breathe in.

   Relaxing my body, I breathe out.

   Aware of body / Relaxing body

6 Calming my body, I breathe in.

   Caring for my body, I breathe out.

   Calming / Caring

7 Smiling to my body, I breathe in.
   Releasing the tension in my body,
   I breathe out.
   Smiling to body / Releasing tension

8 Breathing in, I calm my body.
   Breathing out, I smile.
   Calm / Smile

9 Breathing in, I dwell in the present moment.
   Breathing out, I know it is a wonderful moment.
   Present moment / Wonderful moment

SITTING WITH THE BUDDHA

When you sit on your own, you may like to think of the Buddha as sitting with you. You can say, "Dear Buddha, I invite you to sit with me. Please make good use of my back. My back is still good enough. And I know that when you sit, you will make my back upright and relaxed. When you breathe, I know your quality of breathing is very good. Use my lungs to breathe and my back to sit." The Buddha isn't someone outside of you. Inside each one of us there are seeds of mindfulness, peace, and enlightenment. When you sit, you give these seeds a chance to manifest. When you invite the Buddha in you to sit, he will sit beautifully right away. You don't have to do anything, just enjoy his sitting and his breathing. You can say these words to yourself as you follow your breath:

Let the Buddha breathe.
Let the Buddha sit.
I don't have to breathe.
I don't have to sit.

When you find yourself in a difficult situation or you are feeling too upset or restless to sit, ask the Buddha to do it for you. Then it becomes easy. The next exercise is:

The Buddha is breathing.
The Buddha is sitting.
I enjoy breathing.
I enjoy sitting.

The next verse is:

> Buddha is breathing.
> Buddha is sitting.
> I am breathing.
> I am sitting.

In the beginning, you and the Buddha are separate. Then you come closer. The next verse is:

> There is breathing.
> There is sitting.
> No one is breathing.
> No one is sitting.

When the Buddha breathes, the quality of breathing is light and easy. When the Buddha sits, the quality of sitting is perfect.

The Buddha doesn't exist outside of the breathing and the sitting. There is only the breathing and the sitting. There is no breather. There is no sitter. When there is a high quality of breathing or sitting, when thoughts, speech, and action are full of mindfulness and compassion, you know the Buddha is there. There is no Buddha outside of these things. I am breathing. I am sitting. There is the breathing. There is sitting. There is no one breathing. There is no one sitting.

Joy in the breathing.
Peace in the sitting.
Joy is the sitting.
Peace is the breathing.

TALKING WITH YOUR INNER CHILD

As children, we were vulnerable and dependent on others for our survival. You may have had hurts and fears as a child that were not safe to share and that you kept inside. Now, as an adult, you are no longer that vulnerable child. You can take care of yourself. You can protect yourself. But the little child in us continues to worry and to be fearful.

The child you were and the grown-up you are now are not exactly two different people and are not exactly one. The inner child is as real as the grown-up adult. They influence each other, just as a seed of corn is still real inside the cornstalk. This guided meditation is a chance to talk with your inner child, to invite him or her to come out and greet life in the present moment. We can let him or her know there is no need to worry any longer. Everything is okay now.

For this meditation, put two cushions in front of each other. Sit on one cushion and look at the other cushion and visualize yourself as a five-year-old. You can visualize yourself at a younger age if that's more helpful. Then, as you sit and breathe mindfully, you can talk to the vulnerable little child inside you. You may say something like, "My dear child, I know you are there, and I am here for you. If you have something to tell me, please say it to me."

After some moments, allow yourself to speak as that small child, expressing anything you never got a chance to share. You may complain. You may share the feeling of being fragile and helpless. Use any kind of language that feels right to you as that child. When some emotion like fear or anger comes up, that's fine.

Then, give yourself a few moments to breathe mindfully and calm your body. Speak to your inner child again, addressing the fears and anger. Let the child know you've been listening and that now you have grown up and can protect yourself so everything will be okay. In this way, you can bring your inner child and grown-up self together into the here and now and be able to more fully experience and enjoy your life as it is happening right now.

SITTING WITH DEATH

We know that life is impermanent and that sooner or later we all have to die. Sitting meditation is a wonderful way to have more awareness and acceptance of the impermanence of the body. If we can become familiar and comfortable with our fear of dying, we can begin to transform that fear. With our awareness of impermanence, we begin to live our lives more deeply, with more care and awareness. When we can envision and accept our own death, we are able to let go of many ambitions, worries, and sufferings. We are able to let go of all the things that keep us so unnecessarily busy. We can begin to live in a way that's meaningful for ourselves, for other species, and the planet.

Following our breathing, we can say:

> All phenomena are impermanent.
> They are subject to birth and death.
> When the notions of birth and death
> are removed,
> this silence is called great joy.

This meditation sums up all of the Buddha's teaching. The last two lines speak of the thundering silence, which is the silencing of all speculation, philosophies, notions, and ideas.

This meditation reminds us that as long as there is the appearance of phenomena there is birth and death. When we look deeply, we see there is no birth and death. We are like the clouds in the sky, never dying, never passing from being to nonbeing. A cloud can become snow or ice or rain, but a cloud cannot become nothing. A cloud cannot die. If we overcome the notion of birth and death, we are no longer afraid of impermanence.

WRITE YOUR OWN

You can write your own practice verse to best help you produce your true presence and get in touch with your true intention. Choose one element that you want to bring into your life and one element that you want to let go. You can use this gatha in concert with your breath to return to that intention.

Breathing in, _____ (A)

Breathing out, _____ (B)

A. *[In-breath]*

B. *[Out-breath]*

Here are some examples:

Breathing in, I am aware of tension in my body.

Breathing out, I let go of the
tension in my body.
Aware of tension / Letting go of tension

Breathing in, I calm my agitation.
Breathing out, I feel at ease.
Calm / Ease

Breathing in, I'm in touch
with the cool autumn air.
Breathing out, I smile to the
cool autumn air.
Autumn air / Smiling

RELATED TITLES

Awakening Joy
by James Baraz and Shoshana Alexander

Be Free Where You Are by Thich Nhat Hanh

Being Peace by Thich Nhat Hanh

Breathe: A Journal by Thich Nhat Hanh

Breathe, You are Alive! by Thich Nhat Hanh

Calm, Ease, Smile, Breathe by Thich Nhat Hanh

Deep Relaxation by Sister Chan Khong

The Energy of Prayer by Thich Nhat Hanh

Happiness by Thich Nhat Hanh

Making Space by Thich Nhat Hanh

Mindful Movements by Thich Nhat Hanh

Moments of Mindfulness by Thich Nhat Hanh

Peace of Mind by Thich Nhat Hanh

Monastics and visitors practice the art of mindful living in the tradition of Thich Nhat Hanh at our ten mindfulness practice centers around the world. For a full listing of practice centers, or for information about retreats, visit plumvillage.org or contact:

Plum Village
33580 Dieulivol, France
plumvillage.org

Deer Park Monastery
Escondido, CA 92026, USA
deerparkmonastery.org

Magnolia Grove Monastery
Batesville, MS 38606, USA
magnoliagrovemonastery.org

Blue Cliff Monastery
Pine Bush, NY 12566, USA
bluecliffmonastery.org

European Institute of
Applied Buddhism
D-51545 Waldbröl, Germany
eiab.eu

Thailand Plum Village
Nakhon Ratchasima,
30130 Thailand
phfhk.org

The Mindfulness Bell, a journal of the art of mindful living in the tradition of Thich Nhat Hanh, is published three times a year by our community. To subscribe or to see the worldwide directory of Sanghas, or local mindfulness groups, visit mindfulnessbell.org.

The Thich Nhat Hanh Foundation supports Thich Nhat Hanh's peace work and mindfulness teachings around the world. For more information on how you can help or on how to nourish your mindfulness practice, visit the foundation at tnhf.org.

**PARALLAX
PRESS**

Parallax Press, a nonprofit publisher founded by
Zen Master Thich Nhat Hanh, publishes books
and media on the art of mindful living and
Engaged Buddhism. We are committed to offering
teachings that help transform suffering and
injustice. Our aspiration is to contribute to collective
insight and awakening, bringing about a more
joyful, healthy, and compassionate society.

View our entire library at **parallax.org**.

HOW TO
EAT

THICH NHAT HANH

PARALLAX
PRESS

BERKELEY, CALIFORNIA

Parallax Press
P.O. Box 7355
Berkeley, California 94707
www.parallax.org

Parallax Press is the publishing division of
Plum Village Community of Engaged Buddhism, Inc.
Copyright © 2014 Plum Village Community of
Engaged Buddhism, Inc.

Printed by Friesens, Altona, MB, Canada, employee owned
and operated

Cover and text design by Debbie Berne
Illustrations by Jason DeAntonis
Edited by Rachel Neumann

ISBN: 978-1-937006-72-3

Library of Congress Cataloging-in-Publication Data
Nhat Hanh, Thich, author.
  How to eat / Thich Nhat Hanh ; illustrated by Jason
DeAntonis.
    pages cm
  ISBN 978-1-937006-72-3 (paperback)
1. Meditation—Buddhism. 2. Dinners and dining—
Religious aspects—Buddhism. I. Title.
  BQ9800.T5392N45448 2014
  294.3'444—dc23
                                        2014015222

8 9 / 22

CONTENTS

NOTES ON EATING

MINDFUL EATING

To cultivate mindfulness, we can do the same
things we always do—walking, sitting, working,
eating, and so on—with mindful awareness
of what we are doing. When we're eating, we
know that we are eating. When we open a
door, we know that we're opening a door. Our
mind is with our actions.

When you put a piece of fruit into your
mouth, all you need is a little bit of mindfulness
to be aware: "I am putting a piece of apple
in my mouth." Your mind doesn't need to be
somewhere else. If you're thinking of work while
you chew, that's not eating mindfully. When you
pay attention to the apple, that is mindfulness.
Then you can look more deeply and in just a
very short time you will see the apple seed, the

beautiful orchard and the sky, the farmer, the picker, and so on. A lot of work is in that apple!

NOTHING COMES FROM NOTHING

With just a little bit of mindfulness, you can truly see where your bread comes from. It has not come from nothing. Bread comes from the wheat fields, from hard work, and from the baker, the supplier, and the seller. But the bread is more than that. The wheat field needs clouds and sunshine. So in this slice of bread there is sunshine, there is cloud, there is the labor of the farmer, the joy of having flour, and the skill of the baker and then—miraculously!—there is the bread. The whole cosmos has come together so that this piece of bread can be in your hand. You don't need to do a lot of hard work to get this insight. You only need to stop letting your mind carry you away with worrying, thinking, and planning.

YOUR BODY BELONGS
TO THE EARTH

In modern life, people tend to think their
bodies belong to them, that they can do anything they want to themselves. But your body
is not only yours. Your body belongs to your
ancestors, your parents, and future generations. It also belongs to society and to all the
other living beings. The trees, the clouds, the
soil, and every living thing brought about the
presence of your body. We can eat with care,
knowing we are caretakers of our bodies,
rather than their owners.

EATING WITHOUT THINKING

When we eat we usually think. We can enjoy our eating a lot more if we practice not thinking when we eat. We can just be aware of the food. Sometimes we eat and we're not aware that we're eating. Our mind isn't there. When our mind isn't present, we look but we don't see, we listen but we don't hear, we eat but we don't know the flavor of the food. This is a state of forgetfulness, the lack of mindfulness. To be truly present we have to stop our thinking. This is the secret of success.

WAITING WITHOUT WAITING

When we serve ourselves food and then bring it to the table, we don't need to feel we're waiting for other people to serve themselves and be seated. All we have to do is breathe and enjoy sitting. We haven't eaten our meal yet, but we can already feel joy and gratitude. It's an opportunity for us to be peaceful.

Standing in line at a grocery store or a restaurant, or waiting for the time to eat, we don't need to waste our time. We don't need to "wait" for one second. Instead, we can enjoy breathing in and out for our nourishment and healing. We can use that time to notice that we will soon be able to have food, and we can be happy and grateful during that time. Instead of waiting, we can generate joy.

SLOWING DOWN

When we can slow down and really enjoy our food, our life takes on a much deeper quality. I love to sit and eat quietly and enjoy each bite, aware of the presence of my community, aware of all the hard and loving work that has gone into my food. When I eat in this way, not only am I physically nourished, I am also spiritually nourished. The way I eat influences everything else that I do during the day.

Eating is as important a time for meditation as sitting or walking meditation time. It's a chance to receive the many gifts of the Earth that I would not otherwise benefit from if my mind were elsewhere. Here is a verse I like to recite when I eat:

In the dimension of space and time,
We chew as rhythmically as we breathe.
Maintaining the lives of all our ancestors,
Opening an upward path for descendants.

We can use the time of eating to nourish the best things our relatives have passed onto us and to transmit what is most precious to future generations.

PAYING ATTENTION TO JUST TWO THINGS

While we eat, we can try to pay attention to just two things: the food that we're eating and our friends who are sitting around us and eating with us. This is called mindfulness of food and mindfulness of community. Eating mindfully, we become aware of all the work and energy that has gone into bringing the food to us. If we are eating with others, we can notice how wonderful it is that during this sometimes hectic life we can find the time to sit together in a relaxed way like this to enjoy a meal. When you can breathe, sit, and eat together with your family or friends in mindfulness, this is called true community-building.

EACH SPOONFUL CONTAINS THE UNIVERSE

Pay attention to each spoonful of food. As you bring it up to your mouth, use your mindfulness to be aware that this food is the gift of the whole universe. The Earth and the sky have collaborated to bring this spoonful of food to you. While breathing in and out, you only need a second or two to recognize this. We eat in such a way that every morsel of food, every moment of eating has mindfulness in it. It takes only a few seconds to see that the food we're holding in our spoon is the gift of the whole cosmos. While we chew, we maintain that awareness. When we chew, we know that the whole universe is there in that bite of food.

BREATHING COMES FIRST

The first thing to do when you sit down with your bowl of food is to stop the thinking and be aware of your breathing. Breathe in such a way that you are nourished. You are nourished by your breathing and you nourish other people with your practice of breathing. We nourish one another.

TURNING OFF THE TV

Sometimes people eat while watching TV. But
even if you turn off the TV, the TV in your mind
continues to run. So you have to also stop the
TV in your head. If there is thinking still going
on in your mind, you'll be dispersed. To be
truly present you need to not just turn off the
television or radio in your house, you need
to turn off the conversation and images in
your head.

HOW MUCH IS ENOUGH

We don't need to eat a lot to feel nourished.
When we are fully there and alive for every
morsel of food, we eat in a way that each bite
fills us with peace and happiness. If we are full
of this joy, we may find that we naturally feel
satisfied with less food.

PREPARING A MEAL

When you prepare a meal with artful awareness, it's delicious and healthy. You have put
your mindfulness, love, and care into the meal,
then people will be eating your love. People
can fully enjoy the meal with body and mind,
just like you enjoy a beautiful work of art.
Eating is not only nourishing for the body, but
also for the mind.

THE KITCHEN

The kitchen can be a meditative practice space if we practice mindful awareness while we are cooking and cleaning there. We can set an intention to execute our tasks in a relaxed and serene way, following our breathing and keeping our concentration on what we are doing. If we are working with others, we may only need to exchange a few words about the work at hand.

A KITCHEN ALTAR

In your own kitchen, you might want to create a kitchen altar to remind yourself to practice mindfulness while cooking. It can be just a small shelf with enough room for an incense holder and perhaps a small flower vase, a beautiful stone, a small picture of an ancestor or spiritual teacher, or a statue—whatever is most meaningful to you. When you come into the kitchen, you can begin your work by offering incense and practicing mindful breathing, making the kitchen into a meditation hall.

COOKING WITHOUT RUSHING

While cooking, allow enough time so you don't feel rushed. If we are aware that our bodies and those of our loved ones depend on the food we're preparing, this awareness will guide us to cook healthy food infused with our love and mindful attention.

PRACTICING PEACE WHILE CHOPPING VEGETABLES

Peace can be practiced while chopping vegetables, cooking, washing dishes, watering the vegetable garden, and also while driving or working. Practice releasing the tension in body and mind and being completely with your task. The time when you work in the kitchen is also the time for meditation.

SETTING THE TABLE

Eating a meal in mindfulness is an important practice. We turn off the TV, put down our newspaper, and work together for five or ten minutes, setting the table and finishing whatever needs to be done. During these few minutes, we can be very happy. When the food is on the table and everyone is seated, we practice breathing. "Breathing in, I calm my body. Breathing out, I smile," we repeat three times. We can recover ourselves completely after three breaths like this.

COOKING WITH JOY

Cooking can bring us a lot of joy. When I put the water into the basin for washing the vegetables, I look deeply at the water to see its wonderful nature. I see that the water comes from high in the mountains or from deep within the Earth right into our kitchen. I know that there are places where people have to walk several miles just to carry back a pail of water on their shoulders. Here, water is available whenever I turn on the tap. Aware of the preciousness of clean water, I value the water that is available to me. I also value the electricity that I use to turn on a light or to boil water. I only need to be aware that there is water and electricity easily accessible to me, and I can be happy straightaway. When I am peeling vegetables or cooking them, I can do it in mindfulness and with love. I see cooking as a way to offer nourishment and care to my family and friends. I will easily find joy and peace in the work. Looking deeply at a tomato, a bunch of grapes, or a piece of tofu, I can see the wonderful nature of these things, how they were nurtured by the soil, the sun, the rain, and the seed. Try to organize your life so that you have enough time and energy to cook in a leisurely and peaceful way. The energy of love and harmony in the kitchen will penetrate into the food that you're cooking to offer to your loved ones and yourself.

A GRAIN OF RICE CONTAINS THE UNIVERSE

When we look at a grain of rice, one second of mindfulness and concentration allows us to see that this grain contains the whole world— the rain, the cloud, the Earth, time, space, farmers, everything. Mindfulness and concentration bring insight, and suddenly we can see so much in a grain of rice. It's very quick! Wherever there is mindfulness and concentration, there is insight. When you put that grain of rice into your mouth, you are putting the whole universe in your mouth. This is possible when you stop your thinking. When you chew that grain of rice, just chew, so no thinking will cut you off from this wonderful reality.

COMMUNION

In some traditions, monastics want to take their minds off food and focus on the virtues of a spiritual life. In my tradition, we do the opposite. We just focus on the food. We see the food as the cosmos. In the Catholic tradition, in the Eucharist you see the piece of bread as the body of Jesus. In the Buddhist tradition, we see the piece of bread as the body of the cosmos. Everything is there. When you chew it mindfully, without thinking, you can see very well all that the piece of bread contains. That is why when you take a bite of the bread and chew mindfully, you are truly in communion with all of life.

TAKE YOUR TIME

It's good to take time to eat, because the time
for a meal can be a very happy time. Take time
to enjoy your breakfast, lunch, and dinner.
Enjoy your meal. Stop the thinking and be
there fully, body and mind.

AN AMBASSADOR
OF THE COSMOS

When you pick up an ear of corn, take one second to look at it. You can see the Earth, the sunshine, and the rain in the corn. Everything has come together to produce that corn you are holding. So the corn is an ambassador coming to nourish you. It only takes one or two seconds to get that insight. When you put the corn into your mouth, chew it mindfully and greet the universe.

CHEW YOUR FOOD, NOT YOUR WORRIES

Sometimes we eat, but we aren't thinking of our food. We're thinking of the past or the future or mulling over some worry or anxiety again and again. So stop thinking about your business, about the office, or about anything that isn't happening right now. Don't chew your worries, your fear, or your anger. If you chew your planning and your anxiety, it's difficult to feel grateful for each piece of food. Just chew your food.

NOURISHED BY THE PRACTICE

Try to be present with your food and with the people sitting around the table with you. Don't close your eyes or look down while you chew. You can open your eyes and if you are with people, notice them alive and well. When we chew with awareness, we're not just nourished by the food, we're nourished by our practice of mindfulness, peace, and happiness. While we chew, we breathe and we enjoy our breathing and our ability to eat and receive nourishment from our food.

FOOD AS MEDICINE

In the original Five Contemplations as they were recited during the Buddha's time, food was considered to be medicine. But I think that when the Buddha received good food, he also enjoyed it. I don't think he thought of it as just taking medicine. We know the food nourishes our bodies. But we can also appreciate and savor our food.

HEALING

When we eat mindfully, we consume exactly what we need in order to keep our bodies, our minds, and the Earth healthy. When we practice like this, we reduce suffering for ourselves and for others. We begin to heal ourselves and can help heal the world. As a spiritual family and as the human family, we can all help make our lives more sustainable by following this practice.

TURNING OFF THE RADIO

In order to eat with joy, we have to turn off
"Radio NST": Non-Stop Thinking. Even if our
bodies are sitting still while we eat, usually
our minds are racing. In order to truly be present for our meal, we have to stop the constant
internal dialogue. To eat without thinking is
to eat in freedom. We are free because we're
not thinking about the past, the future, and our
projects. We are free to be sitting, whether
alone or with loved ones, and enjoying
our meal.

OUR ANCESTORS
ARE IN THE SOIL

That nut, fruit, vegetable, or grain that you eat
has pulled up nutrition from the soil in order
to grow. In the soil are many people who
have died, have been transformed, and have
become part of the soil. Maybe in this mouthful
of rice are also the bones of many hundreds
of generations as well as many dead leaves,
worms, and animals' bones. Maybe in a previous life you had been there and died there,
and your own bones have disintegrated in that
land. During the time of eating, your practice
is to look deeply into that grain of rice and
enjoy all that has gone into its creation. There
are so many things to enjoy and to discover in
each bite.

EATING MINDFULLY
IS A PRACTICE

When we eat our meal, we should show up
for that meal 100 percent. Eating mindfully is a
practice. If we choose to drink a cup of tea in
mindfulness, the pleasure of drinking tea will
more than double because we are truly there
and the tea is also truly there. Life is real; it's
not a dream when mindfulness is there.

EATING IN SILENCE

Sometimes, it can be helpful to have a silent meal to help us practice mindful eating. That way, we can focus our attention on our breath, the food, and the company around us in order to become fully present in the here and now.

EATING A STRING BEAN

Hold up a string bean and take a moment to see that it is a string bean with the whole world in it. There are clouds, sunshine, the whole Earth, and the hard work of the gardener. When we can see like that, we have wisdom. When we have wisdom, it means that we have mindfulness and concentration. Don't chew your worries, your suffering, or your projects. That's not good for your health. Just chew the string bean.

‹ISHED BY THE
.SENT MOMENT

In our daily activities, we often rush from one thing to another. In between tasks we spend our time planning how we'll accomplish future tasks. In all that hurrying and strategizing, we become isolated from the present moment. Eating is a chance to return to the present moment and stop the rushing and the planning.

HOW THE BUDDHA ATE

Eating meditation is a practice that dates back very far. During his lifetime, the Buddha ate with his community of monks and nuns. Each day they ate together in silence, nourished by the food and by the presence of their brothers and sisters in the practice. I don't think they were worrying about their schedule or about the past or the future. I think they just enjoyed being together and eating well. We can eat like that too.

THE VALUE OF A MEAL

We should reflect deeply on what we buy and what we eat. What we buy and eat can contribute to climate change or it can help stop it. Eating is a chance to nourish our bodies and know that we are not destroying the Earth by doing so.

The value of a meal is not just determined by the amount of money we've spent on the ingredients or on a meal at a restaurant. There is so much hard work that goes into growing, harvesting, distributing, and cooking even a dish of rice. A good meal doesn't have to mean it contains expensive ingredients. The best food is often very simple. There are things the grocery store can't provide us with. No matter how much money you have, you can't buy it.

It's only with mindfulness, concentration, and insight that you can get a truly rich meal.

SITTING WHILE YOU EAT

Sometimes we are rushing so much in our day that we eat only as we're running from one place to another. We eat in our car or as we walk. Please sit when you eat. When you sit, that is a reminder to stop. You have nothing to do, nowhere to go.

ONE MINDFUL BREATH

It takes only one moment to take a mindful in-breath and out-breath before you eat. Bring the mind back to the body. Your body is always available for you. You can bring your attention out of your head and into your body. Before you focus on the food, focus on being present with your body: "Breathing in, I am aware that my body is still there. Breathing out, I smile to my body." This body has been given to us by our parents and those before them. When this body was just born, it was very light. As we grow, we tend to get weighed down by worries and lose our freshness and beauty. Mindful eating helps us regain this freshness, nourishing our spirits as well as our bodies. Eating with appreciation of our own bodies, we eat with more relaxation and joy.

THE RIGHT AMOUNT

When we take a moment to sit and breathe before we eat, we can get in touch with the real hunger in our body. We can discover if we're eating because we're hungry or if we're eating because it's the time to eat and the food is there. If we're paying attention and taking our time, we also know how much to eat. Mindfulness is recognizing what is there in the present moment. What is there is the fact that you are still alive and your health is still there. The food in front of you is available to help nourish your body and keep you healthy.

A SILENT MEAL

Happiness is possible during the meal, and silence helps enormously. You may want to pick one meal a week to eat in silence. A silent meal helps you come back to yourself and arrive in the present moment. A truly silent meal includes turning off the noise in your head as well as finding a quiet place to enjoy your meal. You may like to choose to eat the same meal every week silently. This can be a meal you eat by yourself or, if you have family or friends who want to join you for this meal, that is wonderful. Silence helps you return to your mindful breathing. You can stop the internal mental chatter, relax, breathe, and smile. Such a meal can provide many moments of happiness.

A MEAL AT GOOGLE

When I visited Google, I shared a silent meal
with some of the people who work there.
Afterward, they wrote me and said, "Never
before in that cafeteria have I had a meal that
wonderful. I was so happy. I felt so peaceful.
Nobody said anything in that whole room
full of people. Everybody was quiet from the
beginning to the end of the meal. In the history
of Google, that's the first such meal we've
ever had."

ARRANGING A MEAL

You can arrange your schedule so you have enough time to eat. The place and the food should be appropriate. What we eat is very important. Tell me what you eat and I will tell you who you are. Tell me where you eat, and I will tell you who you are.

We are what we consume. If we look deeply into what and how much we consume every day, we'll come to know our own nature very well. We have to eat, drink, and consume, but if we do it unmindfully, we may destroy our body and our consciousness. A meal is an opportunity to show gratitude to those that came before us and those that will come after we are gone.

EATING IS AN ART

Eating well is an art. It doesn't require fancy cooking, but it does require practice and concentration. Your body is not just yours. It is a gift and a responsibility. To keep it healthy, we need to know how to eat.

CHOOSING WHAT TO EAT

Our way of eating and producing food can be very violent, to other species, to our own bodies, and to the Earth. Or our way of growing, distributing, and eating food can be part of creating a larger healing. We get to choose.

The planet suffers deeply because of the way many of us eat now. Forests are razed to grow grain to feed livestock, and the way the animals are raised pollutes our water and air. A lot of grain and water is also used to make alcohol. Tens of thousands of children die of starvation and malnutrition every day, even though our Earth has the ability to feed us all.

With each meal, we make choices that help or harm the planet. "What shall I eat today?" is a very deep question. You might want to ask yourself that question every morning. You may find that as you practice mindful eating and begin to look deeply at what you eat and drink, your desire for certain foods may change. Your happiness and that of the Earth are intertwined.

A VEGETARIAN DIET

The Food and Agricultural Organization (FAO) of the United Nations proposed that the meat industry be reduced by at least 50 percent in order to save our planet. The simple act of becoming vegetarian can make a difference in the health of our planet.

If you're not able to entirely stop eating meat, you can still decide to make an effort to cut back. By cutting meat out of your diet even five or ten days a month, you're already helping. Try to reduce your consumption by at least 50 percent. This begins to nourish your compassion. If you know that you're living in a way that makes a future possible for your planet, you'll have joy.

THE PLANET IS US

Our food comes from this beautiful planet. The Earth is inside of us, in each morsel of food, in the air we breathe, in the water that we drink and that flows through us. Enjoy being part of the Earth and eat in such a way that allows you to be aware that each bite is deepening your connection to the planet.

BON APPÉTIT!

Before eating, we wish people will have a good appetite. We say "bon appétit," just as before going to sleep we say "good night." In Vietnamese, they say "please have a sweet, delicious sleep." In Vietnamese, the word "delicious" always goes together with the word "healthy." So delicious food must be healthy food. We eat delicious food in order to have strength and good health. Food that is tasty but destroys our bodies and our minds is not healthy.

When you eat with mindfulness, you consume deliciously. If you don't feel happy, if you don't feel good enough, then you have to inquire of those who've practiced a long time, "Can you help me? How can I taste the moment deliciously?"

ATTENTION TO WHAT WE EAT

Before eating, you may see a condiment dish
with red chili peppers. It looks very appealing.
But when you look deeper, you know you are
sensitive to them, and if you eat them they
may affect your digestion. So although they're
delicious, they may not be healthy for you.
Something can be delicious and not healthy,
so we have to be very careful about what we
prepare and what we eat. Healthy is good, but
healthy and not delicious isn't good either. You
have to have both.

BOUND BY A HUNDRED STRINGS

Eating is a practice. The practice must be nourishing for us, for our bodies, and also for our minds. If you eat but you are bound by a hundred strings of worries, anger, irritation, stress, and projects, then these one hundred strings are pulling you in one hundred directions. Your food and your experience of eating will be empty and worthless. So you have to plan properly and have the intention that whenever you eat, you eat in freedom.

MEDITATION AS FOOD

Meditation practice is also a kind of food because it nourishes us. Consider the practice offered by the Buddha to be a kind of food. Any practice must be a kind of food. Walking is like a delicious food. Eating is a delicious food, sitting is a delicious food, and working meditation is also delicious food.

WHAT A BABY EATS

Often when I am giving a talk, a few babies will be in the audience, and some of them will be nursing. The infants don't know what a bell is; they don't understand the word "mindfulness," but they are nourished both by their mother's bodies as well as by the sounds of the bell and the talk. They can feel the collective energy of deep peace as everyone breathes in and out. They are getting many different kinds of nourishing food—the milk from their mothers, the sounds of the bell, and the collective energy of mindfulness all around them.

ORGANIZING A MEAL

We can organize a meal in such a way that it can really be a time of practice. A meal can nourish and heal, be delicious, and also help create a peaceful atmosphere. We have many people who are very good at organizing. They get a lot done during the day. But sometimes they forget to eat! They don't organize their day to include mindful meals. Organizing a meal requires making the time to eat, without distractions and worries. Eat in a way that is relaxing and brings you joy. It doesn't take too much organizing and the results are profound.

EATING AND SMILING

Sitting at the table and eating with other people is a chance to offer an authentic smile of friendship and understanding. It's very easy, but not many people do it. To me, the most important part of the practice is to look at each person and smile. When family or community members sit together and cannot smile at each other, the situation is a very dangerous one. Upon finishing your meal, take a few moments to notice that you have finished, that your bowl is now empty, and your hunger is satisfied. This is another opportunity to smile and be grateful that you have had this nourishing food to eat, supporting you on the path of love and understanding.

EATING WITH CHILDREN IN SILENCE

Sometimes parents who might want to enjoy a silent meal think that their children will not be able to enjoy or participate in the silence. But children are very capable of eating in silence for five, ten, or even twenty minutes and can enjoy it very much.

CULTIVATING COMPASSION

Having the opportunity to sit with our family and friends and enjoy wonderful food is something precious, something not everyone has. Many people in the world are hungry. When I hold a bowl of warm, nutritious food, I know that I'm fortunate, and I feel compassion for all those who don't have enough to eat and who are without friends or family. Right at the dinner table, we can cultivate the seeds of compassion that will strengthen our determination to help hungry and lonely people be nourished.

MINDFUL CONVERSATION AT MEALTIME

I don't recommend that all meals be silent. I think talking to each other is a wonderful way to be in touch. But we have to distinguish between different kinds of talk. Some subjects can separate us, for instance, if we talk about other people's shortcomings. The food that has been prepared carefully will have no value if we let this kind of talk dominate our meal. Instead we can speak about things that nourish our awareness of the food and our being together, cultivating happiness.

Refrain from discussing subjects that can destroy your awareness of the people around you and the food. If someone is thinking about something other than the good food on the table, such as his difficulties in the office or with friends, it means he is losing the present moment and the food. You can help by returning his attention to the meal.

INVITING THE BELL
AT MEALTIME

In our practice centers, we invite the bell three times before eating, and then we eat in silence for about twenty minutes. Eating in silence, we are fully aware of our food's nourishment for body and mind. In order to deepen our practice of mindful eating and support the peaceful atmosphere, we remain seated during this silent period. At the end of this time, two sounds of the bell will be invited. We may then start a mindful conversation with our friends or begin getting up from the table.

THE PURPOSE OF BREAKFAST

A few years ago, I asked some children, "What is the purpose of eating breakfast?" One boy replied, "To get energy for the day." Another said, "The purpose of eating breakfast is to eat breakfast." I think the second child is more correct. The purpose of eating is to eat.

A FULL LIFE

If we feel empty, we don't need to go to the refrigerator to take things out to eat. When you eat like that it's because there is a feeling of emptiness, loneliness, or depression inside. The moments of our daily lives can be filled with joy and meaningful activities. Our community includes our family and friends and our connection to other living beings. They are there to help us get out of these feelings. We are not alone. Sharing a meal together is not just to sustain our bodies and celebrate life's wonders, but also to experience freedom, joy, and the happiness of being in a harmonious community during the whole time of eating.

GETTING SUPPORT

Suppose you have trouble with eating. You eat more than you need to and that has brought you a lot of difficulties and suffering. One way to return to joyful eating is to make a commitment to eat with others who support you. Taking refuge in your community can help a lot. We all need a community to help us in our practice. Even if you live alone and don't have a community to practice with, you are not really alone. Many hands have gone into making the food you're eating. There are the microbes and bacteria and other microscopic living things that are in your food, in you, and all around you. Your ancestors as well as your descendants are with you in every cell of your being.

TRULY SEEING

When we look at the people we're eating with, we can see them fully in just a few moments. We don't need two hours to be able to see another person. If we are really settled within ourselves, we only need to look for a few seconds, and that is enough to see our friend. I think that if a family has five members, only about five or ten seconds is needed to practice this "looking and seeing."

ENJOYING DISHWASHING

As novices, we had to wash dishes for one
hundred monks. There was no running water—
no cold water, no hot water, no tap water at
all, and no soap. You may wonder how we
managed to wash the dishes! We had only
ashes, rice husks, and a coconut skin to use as
a sponge. Many people in my country still use
this. You take a layer of coconut skin and dry
it to make into implements for cleaning pots
and pans. We had to heat up a big pot of water
before we could do any scrubbing. As a novice,
I had to go out and gather wood in the pine-
covered hills. We gathered dead branches and
pine needles into a big heap. You can cook
rice or soup with just pine needles.

We were just two novices washing the dishes for one hundred monks. It was a lot of fun washing dishes together, even without hot running water and soap. Some countries have modern homes that are very comfortable. The water, hot and cold, comes right into the kitchen; you have only to turn on the tap.

You can stand there and enjoy washing dishes. But maybe you are lazy. You see a big pile of dishes and you don't want to go over and wash them. But as soon as you roll up your sleeves and stand in front of the basin, it is not difficult anymore.

Whether you are living in a modern country, or you have only a well for water, you can still enjoy washing the dishes.

DISHWASHING AS MEDITATION

Suppose the baby Buddha—or the baby Mohammed, the baby Moses, or the baby Jesus—had just been born. You would want to bathe him with clean water. Wash every bowl, every dish as if you are bathing a baby—breathing in, feeling joy; breathing out, smiling.

Every minute can be a holy, sacred minute. Where do you seek the spiritual? You seek the spiritual in every ordinary thing that you do every day. Sweeping the floor, watering the vegetables, and washing the dishes become holy and sacred if mindfulness is there. With mindfulness and concentration, everything becomes spiritual.

DRINKING A CLOUD

Something as simple and ordinary as drinking a cup of tea can bring us great joy and help us feel our connection to the Earth. The way we drink our tea can transform our lives if we truly devote our attention to it.

Sometimes we hurry through our daily tasks, looking forward to the time when we can stop and have a cup of tea. But then when we're finally sitting with the cup in our hands, our mind is still running off into the future and we can't enjoy what we're doing; we lose the pleasure of drinking our tea. We need to keep our awareness alive and value each moment of our daily life. We may think our other tasks are less pleasant than drinking tea. But if we do them with awareness, we may find that they're actually very enjoyable.

Drinking a cup of tea is a pleasure we can give ourselves every day. To enjoy our tea, we have to be fully present and know clearly and deeply that we are drinking tea.

When you lift your cup, you may like to breathe in the aroma. Looking deeply into your tea, you see that you are drinking fragrant plants that are the gift of Mother Earth. You see the labor of the tea pickers; you see the luscious tea fields and plantations in Sri Lanka, China, and Vietnam. You know that you are drinking a cloud; you are drinking the rain. The tea contains the whole universe.

SNACK MEDITATION

A young friend once asked me to teach him about the practice of mindfulness. I offered him a tangerine, but he continued telling me about his many projects—his work for peace, social justice, and so on. While he was eating, he was thinking and talking. He peeled the tangerine and tossed the sections into his mouth and quickly chewed and swallowed.

I said, "Jim, stop! Eat your tangerine." He looked at me and understood. So he stopped talking and began to eat much more slowly and mindfully. He separated each of the remaining sections, smelled their beautiful fragrance, put one section at a time into his mouth, and felt all the juices surrounding his tongue. What is the purpose of eating a tangerine? It is to eat the tangerine. During the time you eat a tangerine, eating that tangerine is the most important thing in your life.

The next time you have a tangerine, please put it in the palm of your hand and look at it in a way that makes the tangerine real. You don't need a lot of time; just two or three seconds is enough. Looking at it, you will see the beautiful tangerine blossom with sunshine and rain, and the tiny tangerine fruit forming. You can see the baby fruit grow and its color change from green to orange. Peeling the tangerine, smelling and tasting it, you can be very happy. Everything we do can be like this. Whether planting lettuce, washing dishes, writing a poem, or adding columns of numbers, we can do it with concentration and awareness.

THE RIGHT AMOUNT

Mindfulness of eating helps us to know what and how much we should eat. We should take only what we can eat. We tend to ignore the rule of moderation. Many of us should take less than what we're used to eating every day. We see that people who consume less are healthier and more joyful, and that those who consume a lot may suffer very deeply. If we chew carefully, if we eat only what is healthy, then we won't bring sickness into our body or our mind.

SNACKING

If we are hungry, a little snack can be very satisfying. But often we develop a habit of eating a snack whenever we feel loneliness or anxiety. A mindful breath is a good way for your body to "snack" on some mindfulness and recognize and embrace strong feelings that may be there. After a mindful breath, you may have less desire to go and fill up with a snack to distract yourself. Your body is nourished by your breath.

EATING OUR FEELINGS

We human beings have many feelings, both positive and negative. Some people tend to eat more when they're joyful, while others tend to eat less. Some people eat when they are sad or upset as a way of eating their feelings, hoping the feelings will go away. Food becomes a craving then, rather than a source of nourishment. If we don't attempt to look deeply to understand our craving, it will grow. When we take the time to take care of our emotions with mindfulness and compassion, then we can just eat. We can enjoy our food without craving and develop a healthy and positive relationship to eating.

NOURISHING OURSELVES WITH MINDFULNESS

We all know that sometimes we open the refrigerator and take out an item that is not good for our health. We are intelligent enough to recognize that. But still we go ahead and eat it to try to cover up the uneasiness within ourselves—we consume to forget our worries and our anxieties and to repress negative energies like fear and anger. Instead of consuming when a feeling of anxiety comes up, invite the energy of mindfulness to manifest. Practice mindful walking and mindful breathing to generate the energy of mindfulness, and invite that energy up to take care of the energy that's making you suffer. If we can practice like this, we'll have enough of the energy of mindfulness to take care of our fear, our anger, and other negative energies.

MINDFUL CONSUMPTION IS FOR EVERYONE

Eating mindfully is a practice that supports ourselves, our families, our society, and the planet, and it is something everyone of any age can do. Leaders of organizations and communities can model responsible and compassionate eating. If you are a mayor, a governor, or a president, you may want to encourage the people you govern to engage in mindful consumption so that you can reduce the violence and suffering in your community.

THE JOY OF EATING

Eating should be very joyful. When I pick up
my food with my chopsticks, with my spoon
or fork, or with my hands, I take time to look
at it for a moment before I put it in my mouth.
If I am really present, I will recognize the food
right away, whether it is an apple, a radish, or a
piece of potato. I smile to it, put it in my mouth,
and chew with complete awareness of what I
am eating. I chew my food in such a way that
life, joy, solidity, and nonfear become possible.
After eating, I feel nourished, not only
physically, but also mentally and spiritually.

CONTEMPLATIONS
FOR EATING

CONTEMPLATING OUR MEAL

Contemplating our food for a few moments before eating can bring us much happiness. We look at the food in a way that the food becomes real. We think about all the people, animals, plants, and minerals and all the conditions that brought the food to our plate. The food reveals our connection with the Earth and all beings. We remember our determination to eat in a way that preserves our health and well-being and the health and well-being of the Earth. The following contemplations and verses can help us practice mindfulness while eating.

PRACTICING WITH THE FIVE CONTEMPLATIONS

The Five Contemplations can be said before a meal to remind us to be fully present for our meal and enjoy it. You can print them out and read them aloud, or you can memorize them. Then they become truly a part of your meal.

But the Five Contemplations aren't just for reading or reciting before the meal. Otherwise, they can become like something we simply check off before we eat, but then we continue to eat as we always have, carried away by our thinking. Throughout the meal, try to live the Five Contemplations. When you practice eating mindfully, you are worthy of the food. The food that has come to your plate is the result of a lot of love and hard work.

THE FIVE CONTEMPLATIONS

1. This food is a gift of the Earth, the sky, numerous living beings, and much hard and loving work.

2. May we eat with mindfulness and gratitude so as to be worthy to receive this food.

3. May we recognize and transform unwhole-some mental formations, especially our greed, and learn to eat with moderation.

4. May we keep our compassion alive by eating in such a way that reduces the suffering of living beings, stops contributing to climate change, and heals and preserves our precious planet.

5. We accept this food so that we may nurture our brotherhood and sisterhood, build our community, and nourish our ideal of serving all living beings.

A GIFT OF THE EARTH

THE FIRST CONTEMPLATION: *This food is a gift of the Earth, the sky, numerous living beings, and much hard and loving work.*

The first contemplation makes us aware that our food comes directly from the Earth and sky. It is a gift of the Earth and sky, and also of the people who prepared it. There is a lot of loving work that goes into making a meal. This contemplation puts you in touch with the insight that the one contains the all. When you pick up a carrot, you can see right away that the Earth, the sky, and the whole universe have come together to make that wonderful carrot. Many people have done a lot of loving work and many elements have come together to bring that carrot to your plate. When you put it in your mouth, you can be in touch with the whole universe. A bunch of beets, a head of lettuce, and a loaf of bread all help you to be in touch with the love, hard work, and difficulties that brought the food to you. Even if you are eating by yourself, you are not alone. You are part of a larger community that helped grow the food. In your food you can see the precious presence and work of so many people.

GRATITUDE

THE SECOND CONTEMPLATION: *May we eat with mindfulness and gratitude so as to be worthy to receive this food.*

The second contemplation is about being aware of our food's presence and being thankful for having it. We can't allow ourselves to get lost in the past or the future. We are there for the food and our food is there for us; it is only fair. Eat in mindfulness and you will be worthy of the Earth and the sky.

When we look deeply at the work that goes into growing and preparing our food, gratitude comes naturally. So many hands have been part of bringing our food to the table. Eating mindfully is a way of showing appreciation for all the hard work that has gone into manifesting this meal.

EATING WITH MODERATION

THE THIRD CONTEMPLATION: *May we recognize and transform unwholesome mental formations, especially our greed, and learn to eat with moderation.*

The third contemplation is about becoming aware of our negative tendencies and not allowing them to carry us away. We need to learn how to eat in moderation, to eat the right amount of food. It is very important not to overeat. If you eat slowly and chew very carefully, you will get plenty of nutrition. The right amount of food is the amount that helps us stay healthy.

The Buddha was always reminding his monks to eat with moderation. To eat with moderation means to have a light, healthy body. Many illnesses come to us through our mouths. So we want to look into what we eat, and know what we should eat and what we should not eat. Look with the eye of the Buddha. The quality of the food and the quantity of the food is very important. Every monk and nun traditionally has an alms bowl, which is called "the vessel of appropriate measure." It helps them know how much food to take. When they're offered too much food during the almsround, they give some of it to others. So the bowl helps a lot. We know exactly what quantity of food we want to consume, as well as the quality.

EATING TO REDUCE SUFFERING

THE FOURTH CONTEMPLATION: *May we
keep our compassion alive by eating in such
a way that reduces the suffering of living
beings, stops contributing to climate change,
and heals and preserves our precious planet.*

The fourth contemplation is about the quality
of our food. We are determined to ingest only
food that has no toxins for our body and our
consciousness, food that keeps us healthy
and nourishes our compassion. When you eat
in such a way that you can keep compassion
alive in you, that is mindful eating.

Sometimes, even if we're not hungry, we
eat to cover up the suffering inside. We can
eat in a way that doesn't cover up suffering
but acknowledges it and helps it transform.

You may even smile to your own suffering, because suffering has a role to play in helping us transform. Awareness of suffering plays a very important role in helping us to understand suffering and generate the energy of compassion. With mindfulness we're no longer afraid of suffering and pain. We learn how to make good use of the mud of suffering to fabricate lotus flowers.

NURTURING ALL BEINGS

THE FIFTH CONTEMPLATION: *We accept this food so that we may nurture our brotherhood and sisterhood, build our community, and nourish our ideal of serving all living beings.*

The fifth contemplation reminds us to be aware that we receive food in order to realize something. Our lives should have meaning, and that meaning is to help people suffer less and help them to touch the joys of life. When we have compassion in our hearts and we know that we are able to help a person suffer less, life begins to have more meaning. This is an important source of nourishment for us and can bring us a lot of joy. One individual is capable of helping many living beings. This is something we can do wherever we are.

SIX FOOD CONTEMPLATIONS FOR YOUNG PEOPLE

It's wonderful for families to experience the happiness of sitting and eating mindfully together. These Six Contemplations were written particularly to be shared with young people before a meal, but they can be enjoyed by anybody.

1. This food is the gift of the whole universe: the Earth, the sky, the rain, and the sun.

2. We thank the people who have made this food, especially the farmers, the people at the market, and the cooks.

3. We only put on our plate as much food as we can eat.

4. We want to chew the food slowly so that we can enjoy it.

5. This food gives us energy to practice being more loving and understanding.

6. We eat this food in order to be healthy and happy, and to love each other as a family.

SERVING FOOD

In this food

I see clearly

the presence of the entire universe

supporting my existence.

This verse helps us see that our life and the lives of all species are interrelated. Eating is a very deep practice. As you wait to serve yourself or be served, look at the food and smile to it. It contains sunshine, clouds, the sky, the Earth, the farmer, everything.

Look at a peach deeply. Don't put it into your mouth right away. Look at it and smile to it, and if you are mindful you will see the sunshine inside the peach. A cloud is inside. The great Earth is inside. A lot of love and a lot of hard work are inside. Then, when you eat it, please be sure to chew only the peach, and not your projects or your worries. Enjoy eating your peach. The peach is a miracle. You, also, are a miracle. So spend time with your food; every minute of your meal should be happy. Not many people have the time and the opportunity to sit down and enjoy a meal like that. We are very fortunate.

LOOKING AT YOUR PLATE

This plate of food,

so fragrant and appetizing,

also contains much suffering.

This verse has its roots in a Vietnamese folk-song. When we look at our plate, filled with fragrant and appetizing food, we should be aware of the bitter pain of people who suffer from hunger. Every day, thousands of children die from hunger and malnutrition. Looking at our plate, we can see Mother Earth, the farm workers, and the tragedy of the unequal distribution of food.

We who live in North America and Europe are accustomed to eating foods imported from other countries, whether it is coffee from Colombia, chocolate from Ghana, or fragrant rice from Thailand. Many children in these countries, except those from rich families, never see the fine products that are put aside for export in order to bring in money. Some parents are so poor and starving they have to sell their children as servants to families who have enough to eat.

Before a meal, we can join our palms in mindfulness and think about those who do not have enough to eat. Slowly and mindfully, we breathe three times and recite this gatha, or verse. Doing so will help us maintain mindfulness. May we find ways to live more simply in order to have more time and energy to change the system of injustice that exists in the world.

BEGINNING TO EAT

With the first mouthful, I practice
    the love that brings joy.
With the second mouthful, I practice
    the love that relieves suffering.
With the third mouthful, I practice
    the joy of being alive.
With the fourth mouthful, I practice
    equal love for all beings.

During the time we eat the first mouthful,
we express our gratitude by promising to
bring joy to at least one person. With the
second mouthful, we can promise to help
relieve the pain of at least one person. With
the third mouthful, we are in touch with the
wonders of life. With the fourth mouthful,

we practice inclusiveness and the love that is characterized by nondiscrimination. After this, we get in touch with the food and its deep nature.

LOOKING AT YOUR EMPTY BOWL

My bowl, empty now,

will soon be filled with precious food.

Beings all over the Earth are struggling to live.

How fortunate we are to have enough to eat.

When many people on this Earth look at an empty bowl, they know their bowl will continue to be empty for a long time. So the empty bowl is as important to honor as the full bowl. We are grateful to have food to eat and we can find ways to help those who are hungry.

FINISHING YOUR MEAL

My bowl is empty.

My hunger is satisfied.

I vow to live

for the benefit of all beings.

After eating, don't rush on to the next thing. Instead, spend a moment being grateful for the food you have just eaten and all that came together to create this moment. Sometimes we show our gratitude only before we eat, and then after the meal we move on. But we are as grateful for having eaten and for feeling satisfied as we are in the moments of contemplation before we eat. Living peacefully and happily is the best way to show our gratitude and is our greatest gift for the world and the next generation.

HOLDING YOUR CUP OF TEA

This cup of tea in my two hands,
mindfulness is held perfectly.
My mind and body dwell
in the very here and now.

Wherever you are drinking your tea, whether at work or in a café or at home, it is wonderful to allow enough time to appreciate it. If the weather is cold, you can feel the warmth of the cup in your hands. Breathe in and recite the first line; breathe out and recite the second. The next inhalation is for the third line, and the next exhalation is for the fourth line. Breathing mindfully in this way, we recuperate ourselves and the cup of tea reclaims its highest place. If we're not mindful, it's not tea that we're drinking but our own illusions and afflictions. If the tea becomes real, we become real. When we are able to truly meet the tea, at that very moment we are truly alive.

BATHING A BABY

Washing the dishes
is like bathing a baby Buddha.
The profane is the sacred.
Everyday mind is Buddha mind.

When you are cleaning the kitchen or washing the dishes, do it as if you were cleaning an altar or washing a baby. Washing in this way, joy and peace can radiate within and around you. The idea that doing dishes is unpleasant can occur to us only when we are not doing them. Once we're standing in front of the sink with our sleeves rolled up and our hands in warm water, it's really not bad at all. I enjoy taking my time with each dish, being fully aware of the dish, the water, and each movement of my hands. I know that if I hurry in order to go and have dessert or a cup of tea, the time of dishwashing will be unpleasant. That would be a pity, because the dishes themselves and the fact that I am here washing them are both miracles!

If I am incapable of washing dishes joyfully, if I want to finish them quickly so I can go and have dessert and a cup of tea, I will be equally incapable of doing these other things joyfully. With the cup in my hands, I will be thinking about what to do next, and the fragrance and flavor of the tea, together with the pleasure of drinking it, will be lost. I will always be dragged into the future, never able to live in the present moment. The time of dishwashing is as important as any other time.

COMPOSTING OUR FOOD SCRAPS

In the garbage, I see a rose.
In the rose, I see the garbage.
Everything is in transformation.
Even permanence is impermanent.

Whenever we throw food in the compost, it can smell bad. Rotting organic matter smells especially badly. But it can also become rich compost for fertilizing the garden. The fragrant rose and the stinking garbage are two sides of the same existence. Without one, the other cannot be. Everything is in transformation. The rose that wilts after six days will become a part of the compost. After six months the compost is transformed into a rose.

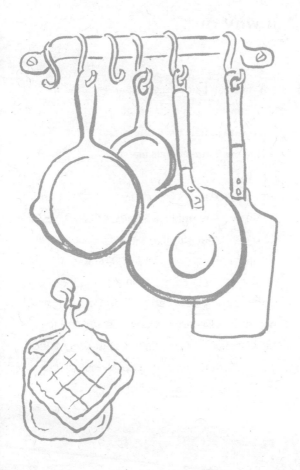

A WAY OUT

I know the Earth is my Mother,
a great living being.
I vow to protect the Earth,
and the Earth protects me.

We practice eating mindfully not just to heal ourselves and our loved ones, but as a way to help the world out of the difficult situation we are in. We become aware of what to consume and what not to consume in order to keep our bodies, our minds, and the Earth healthy, and not to cause suffering for ourselves and for others. Mindful consumption is the way out of our difficulties, not just our personal difficulties, but also the way out of war, poverty, and climate crisis. The Earth requires now that we consume mindfully if we are to survive and thrive as a species.

RELATED TITLES

Awakening Joy
by James Baraz and Shoshana Alexander

Be Free Where You Are by Thich Nhat Hanh

Being Peace by Thich Nhat Hanh

Breathe, You are Alive! by Thich Nhat Hanh

The Cosmos in a Carrot by Carmen Yuen

Deep Relaxation by Sister Chan Khong

Happiness by Thich Nhat Hanh

How to Sit by Thich Nhat Hanh

Making Space by Thich Nhat Hanh

Small Bites by Annabelle Zinser

Moments of Mindfulness by Thich Nhat Hanh

Ten Breaths to Happiness by Glen Schneider

Monastics and visitors practice the art of mindful living in the tradition of Thich Nhat Hanh at our ten mindfulness practice centers around the world. For a full listing of practice centers, or for information about retreats, visit plumvillage.org or contact:

Plum Village
33580 Dieulivol, France
plumvillage.org

Deer Park Monastery
Escondido, CA 92026, USA
deerparkmonastery.org

Magnolia Grove Monastery
Batesville, MS 38606, USA
magnoliagrovemonastery.org

Blue Cliff Monastery
Pine Bush, NY 12566, USA
bluecliffmonastery.org

European Institute of
Applied Buddhism
D-51545 Waldbröl, Germany
eiab.eu

Thailand Plum Village
Nakhon Ratchasima,
30130 Thailand
phfhk.org

The Mindfulness Bell, a journal of the art of mindful living in the tradition of Thich Nhat Hanh, is published three times a year by our community. To subscribe or to see the worldwide directory of Sanghas, or local mindfulness groups, visit mindfulnessbell.org.

The Thich Nhat Hanh Foundation supports Thich Nhat Hanh's peace work and mindfulness teachings around the world. For more information on how you can help or on how to nourish your mindfulness practice, visit the foundation at tnhf.org.

PARALLAX
PRESS

Parallax Press, a nonprofit publisher founded by
Zen Master Thich Nhat Hanh, publishes books
and media on the art of mindful living and
Engaged Buddhism. We are committed to offering
teachings that help transform suffering and
injustice. Our aspiration is to contribute to collective
insight and awakening, bringing about a more
joyful, healthy, and compassionate society.

View our entire library at **parallax.org**.

HOW TO
WALK

THICH NHAT HANH

**PARALLAX
PRESS**

BERKELEY, CALIFORNIA

Parallax Press
P.O. Box 7355
Berkeley, California 94707
parallax.org

Parallax Press is the publishing division of
Plum Village Community of Engaged Buddhism, Inc.

Printed by Friesens, Altona, MB, Canada, employee owned
and operated

Cover and text design by Debbie Berne
Illustrations by Jason DeAntonis
Edited by Rachel Neumann

ISBN: 978-1-937006-92-1

Library of Congress Cataloging-in-Publication Data

Nhat Hanh, Thich, author.
 How to walk / Thich Nhat Hanh.
    pages cm
 ISBN 978-1-937006-92-1 (paperback)
1. Meditation—Buddhism. 2. Walking—Religious
aspects—Buddhism. I. Title.
 BQ5612.N4745 2015
 294.3'4435—dc23
                                    2015005347

7 / 22

CONTENTS

The first thing to do is to lift your foot. Breathe in. Put your foot down in front of you, first your heel and then your toes. Breathe out. Feel your feet solid on the Earth. You have already arrived.

We frequently walk with the sole purpose of getting from one place to another. But where are we in between? With every step, we can feel the miracle of walking on solid ground. We can arrive in the present moment with every step.

When we first learned to walk, we walked just to enjoy walking. We walked and discovered each moment as we encountered it. We can learn to walk that way again.

NOTES ON WALKING

YOU HAVE ARRIVED

When you walk, arrive with every step. That is walking meditation. There's nothing else to it.

WHY WALK?

People ask me, "Why do you do walking meditation?" The best answer I can give is, "Because I like it." Every step makes me happy. There's no use in doing walking meditation if you're not going to enjoy every step you make; it would be a waste of time. The same thing is true with sitting meditation. If someone asked, "What's the use of sitting for hours and hours?" The best answer is, "Because I like sitting." Sitting and walking can bring peace and joy. We have to learn how to sit and walk so that we can produce peace and joy during the time of sitting or the time of walking. We have to learn to walk so that we can enjoy every step. Mindfulness and concentration can bring a higher quality to our breath, to our sitting, and to our steps.

ARRIVING

One of the most profound teachings is also the shortest: "I have arrived." When we return to our breathing, we return to the present moment, our true home. There's no need for us to struggle to arrive somewhere else. We know our final destination is the cemetery. Why are we in a hurry to get there? Why not step in the direction of life, which is in the present moment? If we practice walking meditation for even a few days, we will undergo a deep transformation and learn how to enjoy peace in each moment. We smile, and countless beings throughout the cosmos smile back at us—our peace is so deep. Everything we think, feel, and do has an effect on our ancestors and future generations and reverberates throughout the cosmos.

PRACTICING JOY

We may think of joy as something that happens spontaneously. Few people realize that it needs to be cultivated and practiced in order to grow. Mindfulness is the continuous practice of deeply touching every moment of daily life. To be mindful is to be truly present with your body and your mind, to bring harmony to your intentions and actions, and to be in harmony with those around you. We don't need to make a separate time for this outside of our daily activities. We can practice mindfulness in every moment of the day as we walk from one place to another. When we walk through a door, we know that we're going through a door. Our minds are with our actions.

WALKING ON PLANET EARTH

Walking on this planet is a very wonderful thing to do. When astronauts return to Earth, one of the things that they're most happy to do is to take a walk. Coming back to their home, they can enjoy the grasses, the plants, the flowers, the animals, and the birds with each step. How long do you think they enjoy walking on the Earth after they've returned from space? I'd guess that the first ten days are wonderful. But eventually they get used to it, and maybe a year later they don't feel as happy as they did in the first few months after coming home. Every time we take a step on this Earth, we can appreciate the solid ground underneath us.

I WALK FOR YOU

Many of my ancestors and many of my friends from my generation have already passed away. A good friend of mine is in a wheelchair and can't walk. Another friend has such pain in his knees that he can't walk up and down stairs. So I walk for them. When I breathe in, I say to myself, "It's wonderful that I am still able to walk like this." With that awareness, I can enjoy every step. I say, "I am alive!" Mindfulness reminds me to notice and enjoy that my body is alive and strong enough for me to walk.

SLEEPWALKING

We're in such a rush, looking for happiness
in one place and then another. We walk like
sleepwalkers, without any enjoyment of what
we are actually doing. We are walking, but in
our minds we are already doing something
else: planning, organizing, worrying. There is
no more need to run. Every time we return our
attention to our breath and our steps, it's as
if we wake up. Every step brings us back to
the here and the now. We can touch the Earth
and see the sky and notice all the wonders in
between. In each step there is the possibility
of mindfulness, concentration, and insight.

ENLIGHTENMENT

To enjoy walking meditation isn't difficult at all. You don't need ten years of practicing mindful walking to be enlightened. You need only a few seconds. You just need to become aware that you're walking. Awareness is already enlightenment. Each of us is capable of being mindful of our in-breath and our out-breath. When you breathe in, be aware that you're breathing in. Be aware that you have a body, that you're breathing in and nourishing that body. Be aware that your feet are strong enough for you to enjoy walking. That is also enlightenment. When you breathe out, be aware of the air leaving your body. Be aware that you are alive. This awareness can bring you so much happiness.

WALKING IN THE AIRPORT

When I go to the airport, I like to arrive early
so that I can do walking meditation before the
flight. About thirty years ago I was walking in
the Honolulu airport. Someone came up to me
and asked, "Who are you; what is your spiritual
tradition?" I said, "Why do you ask?" And he
said, "Because I see that the way you walk is
so different than the way others walk. It's so
peaceful and relaxed." He had approached me
simply because of the way I walked. I hadn't
given a speech or a conference. With every
step you make, you can create peace within
yourself and give joy to other people.

CLIMBING THE MOUNTAIN

I once traveled with a delegation to China and climbed Wutai Shan, a famous mountain there. The path to the top is very steep, and usually people arrive exhausted. There are 1,080 steps to climb. Before setting out, I suggested our delegation breathe, make a step, relax; breathe, make another step, and relax. Our intention was to climb the mountain in a way that we could enjoy each moment of the climbing. Every ten steps or so we would sit down, look around, breathe, and smile. We didn't need to arrive; we arrived in every step, with peace, stillness, solidity, and freedom. When we got to the top, everybody was so happy and full of energy. Every step, even uphill, can bring mindfulness, concentration, joy, and insight.

WALKING WITH
DANIEL BERRIGAN

One day in New York City, I invited Daniel
Berrigan, the Catholic father, poet, and peace
activist, to go for a walk in Central Park. I
told him, "No talking, just walking." Father
Berrigan is much taller than I am and his legs
are very long; one of his steps was equal
to two of mine. We started out together but
after a few steps he was way ahead. When he
turned around and saw I wasn't next to him,
he stopped and waited. I didn't rush. I was
determined to walk slowly and mindfully at
my own pace. I was determined to pay close
attention to my steps and breath, otherwise I
knew I would lose myself and get carried away
in the idea that there was a rush. Each time I
caught up, we would walk together for a little
while and then he would get in front again.

Each time, I would keep my own pace. Later, he came to visit me in France and he had a chance to learn and practice walking meditation. He was able to walk without rushing, even when he returned to New York.

WALKING IN BEAUTY

You can walk mindfully on the busiest street. Sometimes, though, it's helpful to practice in a park or some other beautiful, quiet place. Walk slowly, but not so slowly that you draw too much attention to yourself. This is a kind of invisible practice. Enjoy nature and your own serenity without making others uncomfortable or making a show of it. If you see something that you want to stop and appreciate—the blue sky, the hills, a tree, or a bird—just stop, and continue to breathe in and out mindfully. If we don't continue to breathe consciously, sooner or later our thinking will settle back in, and the bird and the tree will disappear.

RUNNING

In every one of us there's a tendency to run.
There's a belief that happiness is not possible
here and now, so we have the tendency to run
into the future in order to look for happiness.
That habit energy may have been transmitted to us by our father, our mother, or our
ancestors. Running has become a habit. Even
in our dreams we continue to run and look for
something. The practice of mindfulness helps
us to stop running and see that everything we
have been looking for is here. Many of us have
been running all our lives. One mindful step
can help us to stop running. When the mind
is focused on breathing and walking, we are
unifying body, speech, and mind, and we are
already home.

PLACE TO PLACE

It is possible to enjoy every step we make, not only during walking meditation, but at any time, whenever you need to move from one place to another place, no matter how short the distance is. If you're walking five steps, then walk those five steps mindfully, feeling your stability with every step. When you climb the stairs, climb each step with joy. With each step, you can generate your best energy and transfer it out into the world.

SILENCE

In Plum Village, the practice center where I live in southwest France, we don't talk when we walk. This helps us fully enjoy walking one hundred percent. If you talk a lot, then it's difficult for you to experience your steps deeply, and you won't enjoy them very much. The same is true when you drink a cup of tea: if you're concentrated and you focus your attention on the cup of tea, then the cup of tea becomes a great joy. Mindfulness and concentration bring about pleasure and insight.

WALKING FOR OUR ANCESTORS AND FUTURE GENERATIONS

All our ancestors and all future generations are present in us all the time. Happiness is not an individual matter. As long as the ancestors in us are still suffering, we can't be happy and we will transmit that suffering to our children and their children. When we walk, we can walk for our ancestors and future generations. Maybe they had to walk with sorrow; perhaps they were forced to march or migrate. When we walk freely, we are walking for them. If we can take one step freely and happily, touching the Earth mindfully, then we can take one hundred steps like that. We do it for ourselves and for all previous and future generations. We all arrive at the same time and find peace and happiness together.

LIFE'S ADDRESS

When you walk mindfully, just enjoy walking. The technique to practice is to walk and just to be exactly where you are, even if you are moving. Your true destination is the here and the now, because only in this moment and in this place is life possible. The address of all the great beings is "here and now." The address of peace and light is also "here and now." You know where to go. Every in-breath, every out-breath, every step you make should bring you back to that address.

INVEST YOUR WHOLE BODY

Invest one hundred percent of yourself into making a step. Touching the ground with your foot, you produce the miracle of being alive. You make yourself real and the Earth real with each step. The practice should be very strong and determined. You are protecting yourself from the habit energy that is always pushing you to run and to get lost in thinking. Bring all your attention down to the soles of your feet, and touch the Earth as though you are kissing the Earth with your feet. Each step is like the seal of an emperor on a decree. Walk as though you imprint your solidity, your freedom, and your peace on the Earth.

STOPPING AND FINDING CALM

Walking is a wonderful way to calm down when we are upset. When we walk, if we focus all our awareness on walking, we are stopping the thinking, storytelling, blaming, and judging that goes on in our heads and takes us away from the present moment. To stop the incessant thinking in the mind, it helps to focus on the body. When things aren't going well, it's good to stop the thinking in order to prevent the unpleasant, destructive energies from continuing. Stopping does not mean repressing; it means, first of all, calming. If we want the ocean to be calm, we don't throw away its water. Without the water, nothing is left. When we notice the presence of anger, fear, and agitation in us, we don't need to throw them away. We only have to breathe in and out consciously and take a mindful step. Allow yourself to sink deeply into the here and the now, because life is available only in the present moment. This alone is enough to calm the storm.

RECOVERING OUR SOVEREIGNTY

When we are pushed and pulled in many different directions, we lose our sovereignty. We're not free. Don't allow yourself to be carried away anymore. Resist. Each mindful step is a step toward freedom. This kind of freedom is not political freedom. It's freedom from the past, from the future, from our worries and our fears.

ONLY WALK

When you walk, only walk. Don't think. Don't talk. If you want to talk to others or have a snack, you can stop in order to do so. In that way, you'll be fully present for the walking and also fully present for the person you're speaking to when you talk. You can sit down somewhere to make your phone call in peace, to eat your food, or drink your juice in mindfulness.

WALKING IS A MIRACLE

Our true home is in the present moment. To live in the present moment is a miracle. When I breathe in and become fully alive, I see myself as a miracle. When I look at an orange mindfully, I see the orange is a miracle. When I peel an orange mindfully, I see that eating an orange is also a miracle. The fact that you are still alive is a miracle. So miracles are the things that you perform several times each day with the power of mindfulness. The miracle is not to walk on water. The miracle is to walk on the green Earth in the present moment, to appreciate the peace and beauty that are available now. I perform this miracle every time I walk. You too can perform the miracle of walking any time you want.

MOTHER EARTH

When we walk, we touch the Earth. It's a great
happiness to be able to touch the Earth, the
mother of all beings on this planet. While practicing walking, we should be aware that we are
walking on a living being that is supporting not
just us, but all of life. A lot of harm has been
done to the Earth, so now it is time to kiss the
ground with our feet, with our love. While you
are walking, smile—be in the here and the
now. By doing so, you transform the place
where you are walking into a paradise.

IMPRINTING ON THE EARTH

We walk all the time, but usually we only walk because we have to, so that we can get to the next thing. When we walk like that, we print anxiety and sorrow on the Earth. We have the capability to walk in a way that we only imprint peace and serenity on the Earth. Every one of us can do that. Any child can do that. If we can take one step like that, we can take two, three, four, and five. When we are able to take one step peacefully, happily, we are creating one more step of peace and happiness for the whole of humankind.

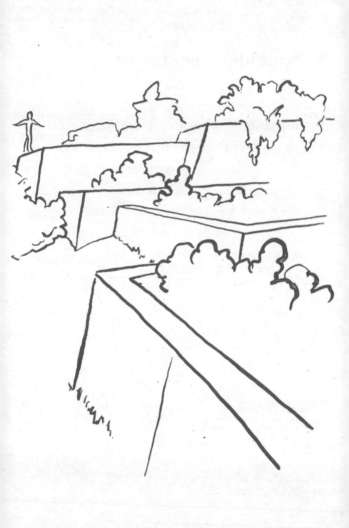

TOUCHING PEACE

The possibility of peace is all around us, in the world and in nature. Peace is also within us, in our bodies and our spirits. The act of walking will water the seeds of peace that are already there inside us. Our mindful steps help us cultivate the habit of touching peace in each moment.

A CONTRACT WITH THE STAIRCASE

Make an agreement with the flight of stairs you use most often. Decide to always practice walking meditation on those stairs, going up and going down; don't climb those stairs absentmindedly. If you commit to this and then realize you have climbed several steps in forgetfulness, go back down and climb up them again. Over twenty years ago, I signed such an agreement with my stairs, and it has brought me great joy.

WALKING ON CAPITOL HILL

Once we offered a retreat for Congress members and staff in Washington, D.C., and some of the participants have continued to practice walking meditation every day. Everyone there walks very quickly, so they have had to be diligent to continue practicing what they learned at the retreat, but a couple of them have kept it up. They told me that they always do walking meditation from their office to the place where they cast their vote. They say they can survive better in their environment because of that kind of practice, even during the most difficult and contentious sessions.

WALKING WITH OTHERS

I have been in crowds of two or three thousand people practicing walking meditation together. It is very powerful. Everybody makes just one step at a time and is wholly concentrated on that step. Please arrange things so that during your day you have many chances to try walking mindfully on your own. You can also practice walking with others to get support. You can ask a friend to go with you. If you're with a child, you can take the hand of the child and walk with him or her.

A KUNG FU NOTEBOOK

The words "kung fu" mean daily diligent practice. You don't have to be doing martial arts
to have a daily practice. Walking can be that
practice. At the end of the day, you might like
to review and write about the practice you've
had during the day, what you noticed about
walking, breathing, smiling, or speaking. It
would be a pity if you spent the whole day
without enjoying walking. You have feet, and
if you don't make use of them it's a loss and
a waste. Someone is telling you now so that
in the future you cannot say: "No one told me
that it was important to enjoy using my feet."

THE FRUIT OF OUR PRACTICE

When you walk with a lot of tenderness and happiness on this beautiful planet, you are living peace. In Buddhist practice, it is said that the *bodhisattva* Avalokiteshvara, a being with great compassion, spends all of his or her time on Earth enjoying walking, riding the waves of birth and death, and smiling. We should be able to do the same. If we can truly arrive and feel at home while walking, that is the practice—but it is also the fruit of our practice. These are moments that are worth living.

PUTTING ON YOUR SHOES

Every day you put on your shoes and walk
somewhere. So every day you have an opportunity to practice mindfulness that doesn't take
any extra time. You take off your shoes and
you put them on. This is also a time for practice and enjoyment.

THE BUDDHA'S FEET

If you empower your feet with the energy of mindfulness, your feet become the Buddha's feet. You may have seen people who walk with the Buddha's feet; you can tell just by watching them. It's very easy. If you have an electric car, it takes a few hours to recharge it. But to empower your feet with the energy of mindfulness, you don't even need half an hour. The power of mindfulness comes right away. It's up to you whether you choose to walk with the feet of the Buddha.

WALKING AND TALKING

Often when we walk, we are already talking
to someone next to us, or thinking of what we
have to do next, or even staring at our phone,
not looking at where we are or where we're
going. When you walk, try to just walk. Try not
to walk and talk at the same time. If you need
to say something, stop altogether and say it.
It won't take too much more time. Then, after
you finish talking, you can resume walking.

WALKING IN PRISON

I have a friend, a nun, who graduated from Indiana University in English literature, and then practiced as a nun in Vietnam. She was arrested by the police and put in prison because of her public calls for peace. She tried her best to practice walking and sitting meditation in her prison cell. It was difficult, because during the daytime, if the guards saw her practicing meditation, they thought of it as a provocative action. She had to wait until they turned off the light in order to practice. She did walking meditation, even though her cell was only ten square feet. In prison, they stole many freedoms from her, but they couldn't steal her determination and her practice.

FINDING EASE

If walking feels difficult or challenging, stop.
Let your breath lead you. Don't force it. Once,
I was in a crowded airport. People were
gathered around me so close that I couldn't
even walk. I couldn't take one step. I started
to push through them, but then I stopped. I
remembered that I didn't have to do anything.
I became so relaxed, because I felt that the
Buddha was walking, not me. If it was me,
maybe I wouldn't have been so relaxed and
compassionate like that. As soon as I stopped
and relaxed, I was able to walk freely. The
airport was still crowded, but I took each step
slowly, with ease and joy.

WALKING FOR OTHERS

Sometimes I say that I walk for my mother or that my father is enjoying walking with me. I walk for my father. I walk for my mother. I walk for my teacher. I walk for my students. Maybe your father never knew how to walk mindfully, enjoying every moment like that. So I do it for him and we both get the benefit.

A LONG WALK

After his enlightenment in Bodhgaya, the Buddha practiced walking meditation around the nearby lotus pond. Then, he wanted to share his insights with his close friends who were in the Deer Park, in Sarnath. So he walked from Bodhgaya to Sarnath to find them. He walked alone among rice fields and forests. It must have taken him at least two weeks to get there, but he enjoyed every step he made. When the Buddha found his old friends, he shared his first teaching.

NIRVANA

Nirvana is something that can't be described. You have to taste it for yourself. If you've never eaten kiwi fruit, no one can describe to you how it tastes. The best way to find out is to put a piece of kiwi in your mouth. Then you'll know the taste of kiwi right away. Nirvana is the same. You have to taste nirvana for yourself. Nirvana is available to you right now in every step. You don't need to die in order to enter into it. It's not vague or far away. If every step you make takes you to the shore of freedom, then you can already taste nirvana.

WALKING HOME

Walking brings the mind and body together.
Only when mind and body are united are we
truly in the here and the now. When we walk,
we come home to ourselves. If you're busy
talking while you walk, or planning ahead, you
won't enjoy your in-breath and out-breath. You
won't enjoy being fully in the present moment.
We don't have to force ourselves to breathe in,
because we're breathing in and out all the time
anyway. We only need to focus our attention
on the breath and the walking. In no time at all,
you go home to your body, and there you are,
well established in the here and the now.

COLLECTIVE ENERGY

When we walk with others, the collective energy of mindfulness we generate is very powerful. It helps heal everyone. When we walk together, producing the energy of mindfulness, going home to the here and the now, we can feel paradise right under our feet; you can see this paradise all around you.

GENERATING MINDFUL ENERGY

When we walk, we produce the energy of mindfulness. Instead of thinking of this or that, just be aware of the contact between your foot and the ground. If you pay attention to that contact, it's very healing. Don't wait until you have a group or a scheduled time. Every time you need to move from one place to another, you can apply the techniques of walking meditation. From your living room to your kitchen, from your car to your work, take your time and enjoy every step. Stop the thinking, stop the talking, and touch the Earth with your feet. If you enjoy every step, your practice is good.

SOLIDITY

When the past and the future can't pull you away anymore, every step is solid. You are firmly established in the here and the now. Solidity and freedom are the foundation of happiness. If you're not solid, if you're not free, happiness isn't possible. So every step is to cultivate more solidity and freedom. As you walk, you can say to yourself, "I am solid. I am free." This is not autosuggestion or wishful thinking. This is a realization, because if you are well established in the here and the now, you realize this truth with every step.

LETTING GO OF THE PAST

Most of us walk without chains, yet we aren't free. We're tethered to regret and sorrow from the past. We return to the past and continue to suffer. The past is a prison. But now you have the key to unlock the door and arrive in the present moment. You breathe in, you bring your mind home to your body, you make a step, and you arrive in the here and the now. There is the sunshine, the beautiful trees, and the songs of the birds.

TAKING CARE OF THE FUTURE

There are those of us who are prisoners of the future. We don't know what will happen but we worry so much that the future becomes a kind of prison. The real future is made only of one substance, and that is the present. What else can the future be made of? If we know how to take care of the present moment the best we can, that's all we can do to assure ourselves of a good future. We build the future by taking care of the present moment. Taking care of the present moment includes mindful breathing, enjoying your in-breath and out-breath. With each step, you arrive in the future you are making. Make it a future of peace and compassion.

LISTEN TO YOUR LUNGS

Let your own lungs determine your breathing. Never force your breath. When walking, match your steps to your breath, not the other way around. You might begin by taking two steps for your in-breath and three steps for your out-breath. If, as you continue to walk, your lungs say they'd be happier making three steps while breathing in and five steps while breathing out, then you make three steps and five steps. Of course when you're climbing a hill, the number of steps you can take with each breath will naturally be reduced. In walking meditation, I notice I usually breathe in for four steps and breathe out for six. But when I climb, I do two steps for each in-breath and three for each out-breath. When it's very steep, I sometimes do one step for every breath in and three, two, or even one for every breath out. We have to adapt. Listening to your body as you walk will help make every step pleasant.

GETTING IN TOUCH

Sometimes when I visit with friends or students from far away, they want to stay in touch. For the last forty years, I haven't used a telephone. Many of us talk a lot on the telephone, but that doesn't mean that we have good communication with the other person. I don't have an email address. But you don't need a phone or a computer to be in touch with me. If you just walk from your home to the bus stop in mindfulness and enjoy every step, we're connected. If you practice mindful breathing and mindful walking, we're connected all the time. When people ask me for my address, I tell them, "It's the here and now."

FORGETFULNESS

We have been living in forgetfulness for many years. Forgetfulness is the opposite of mindfulness. Mindfulness is to remember that life is a wonder; we are here, and we should live our lives deeply. We know that we want to be more present, but very often we don't do it. We need a friend or a teacher to remind us. The Earth can be that teacher. It is always there, greeting your feet, keeping you solid and grounded.

TRAINING OURSELVES

There are those of us who, right in the first
session of mindful walking, can already arrive.
Others of us find it difficult, because the habit
of running is so strong. I remember one day
a journalist from Paris came to interview me.
He was invited to join us in walking meditation
before we had the interview. He suffered very
much during the walk. He reported later that
it was exhausting. He was so used to running
that for him walking mindfully and slowly felt
like hard work! So we have to train ourselves
in walking. We walk in such a way that every
step can help us to stop running the useless
race and get in touch with the wonders of life
that are available in the here and the now.

EACH STEP IS AN
ACT OF RESISTANCE

Every step is a revolution against busyness.
Each mindful step says: "I don't want to run
anymore. I want to stop. I want to live my life. I
don't want to miss the wonders of life." When
you can truly arrive, there is peace in you
because you aren't struggling anymore. Each
footprint has peace in it, it has the mark "here
and now" in it. You may enjoy arriving and
feeling at home for three, four, five, or ten minutes, as long as you like. One hour of practice
already begins the revolution.

ACKNOWLEDGING THE BODY

We have a physical body, which is a wonder. But this physical body will one day disintegrate. That is the truth we have to accept. On the surface, there is birth and death, being and nonbeing. But if you go more deeply, you recognize that you also have a cosmic body that exists outside of birth and death, being and nonbeing. A wave on the ocean doesn't last very long. A wave's physical body lasts five, ten, or twenty seconds. But the wave has her ocean body, because she comes from the ocean and she will go back to the ocean. If you walk mindfully, if your concentration and insight are powerful, with every step you can touch your cosmic body and you will lose all your fear and uncertainty.

CREATING A HABIT
OF MINDFUL WALKING

Every time you need to go somewhere, even if it's a very short distance of three or five steps, you can apply mindful walking. Soon, it will become a habit. You will find that you are walking mindfully to pick up the phone or to make your tea. You may not realize at first why you don't feel rushed or why you are happier when you walk in the door. Cultivating a daily habit of walking meditation is free and it doesn't take any more time than the walking you are already doing.

SETTING AN EXAMPLE

When you walk with mindfulness, you set an example for everyone who sees you, even if you don't realize it. When we see you walking with freedom, with peace, with joy, we may be motivated by the desire to mirror you. Together, without effort, we create more of an atmosphere of peace and happiness.

INTENTION

The intention to enjoy your steps and your breath is not enough; you need mindfulness and insight. If every step you take brings you joy, it's because while making a step you have mindfulness and insight. Without insight, it's impossible for you to enjoy your in-breath and out-breath. You can't force yourself to enjoy your breath or your steps. Breathing mindfully, making steps in awareness, joy comes naturally and easily.

THE SOLE OF YOUR FOOT

You might like to focus your attention on the sole of your foot. Feel the contact between your foot and the ground. You are down there in your foot, not up here in your head. There's a feeling that you are touching the beautiful Mother Earth.

WALKING EVERYWHERE

In the Buddha's time, there were no cars, no trains, no airplanes. From time to time the Buddha used a boat to travel upon or across a river. But mostly he walked. During his forty-five years of teaching, he visited and taught in perhaps fourteen or fifteen countries of ancient India and Nepal. That was a lot of walking. Many of his teachings, many of his insights, came from his time of walking everywhere.

WALKING ALONG THE GANGES

The first time I flew into India, I had fifteen
minutes to contemplate the landscape below
before landing in the city of Patna. I saw the
Ganges River for the first time. As a novice
monk, I had learned of the Ganges with its
sands, which are too numerous to be counted.
Sitting in the airplane, I looked down and I saw
the footprints of the Buddha a little bit everywhere all along the banks of the Ganges River.
It is certain that the Buddha walked back and
forth many times along that river. He walked
like that for forty-five years, bringing his wisdom and compassion and sharing his practice
of liberation with many people, from kings and
ministers to scavengers and the poor.

THE NON-PRACTICE PRACTICE

When the Buddha walked, he didn't seem
to be practicing meditation. He didn't have
access to any special tools; he just had two
feet like the rest of of us, and he enjoyed walking. The best way to practice has the appearance of non-practice, but it's very deep. You
don't make any effort; you don't struggle; you
just enjoy walking. "My practice," the Buddha
said in the Sutra of Forty-Two Chapters, "is
the practice of non-practice, the attainment of
non-attainment." If your practice is natural, if
your practice brings you happiness, that's the
best kind of practice. You don't look like you're
practicing, but you're practicing very deeply.

INTENTION

Walking meditation is a way to practice moving without a goal or intention. Mindful walking simply means walking while being aware of each step and of our breathing. We can even practice mindful breathing and walking meditation in between business appointments or in the parking lot of the supermarket. We can keep our steps slow, relaxed, and calm. There's no rush, no place to get to, no hurry. Mindful walking can release our sorrows and our worries and help bring peace into body and mind.

LOVING THE EARTH

When we're in love with someone or something, there's no separation between ourselves and the person or thing we love. We do
whatever we can for them, and this brings us
great joy and nourishment. When we see the
Earth this way, we will walk more gently on her.

WALKING OUTSIDE

When we open the door and go out into the fresh air, we can be immediately in touch with the air and the Earth and all the elements around us. When we walk, we know we're not stepping on something inanimate. The ground we're walking on is not inert matter. Understanding the Earth in this way, we can walk on the planet with as much respect and reverence as we would walk when in a house of worship or in any sacred space. We can bring our full awareness to each step. Steps like these have the power to save our lives.

MORNING WALK

Every morning when I wake up and get
dressed, I leave my hut and take a walk.
Usually the sky is still dark and I walk gently,
aware of nature all around me and the fading
stars. When I think of the Earth and my ability
to walk on it, I think, "I'm going to go out into
nature, enjoying everything beautiful, enjoying
all its wonders." My heart is filled with joy.

WALKING IN THE CITY

Try to practice mindful walking in your daily
life. When you go to the bus stop, make it into
a walking meditation. Even if your surround-
ings are full of noise and agitation, you can
still walk in rhythm with your breathing. In the
commotion of a big city, you can still walk with
peace, happiness, and an inner smile. This is
what it means to live fully in every moment of
every day of your life.

THE AWARENESS OF LOVE

Walking mindfully, with love and understanding, we can become deeply aware of every single thing on this planet. We notice that the leaves on the trees are a startling light green in spring, a vibrant green in summer, rich yellow, orange, and red in autumn, and then in winter, when the branches are bare, the trees continue to stand tall, strong, and beautiful, harboring life deep inside. Mother Earth receives the fallen leaves and breaks them down to create new nourishment for the tree so that it can continue to grow.

WE DON'T WALK ALONE

When we walk, we're not walking alone. Our parents and ancestors are always walking with us. They're present in every cell of our bodies. So each step that brings us healing and happiness also brings healing and happiness to our parents and ancestors. Every mindful step has the power to transform us and all our ancestors within us, including our animal, plant, and mineral ancestors. We don't walk for ourselves alone. When we walk, we walk for our family and for the whole world.

RETURNING

We don't have to wait until we die to return
to Mother Earth. In fact, we're in the process
of going back to Mother Earth right now.
Thousands of cells in our bodies are dying
each moment, and new ones are being born.
Whenever we breathe, whenever we walk, we
are returning to the Earth.

GRATITUDE

When we do walking meditation, we can take
each step in gratitude and joy because we
know that we're walking on the Earth. We can
walk with gentle steps, in reverence to Mother
Earth who gave us birth and of whom we are
a part. The Earth we're walking on is sacred.
We should be very respectful because we
know we're walking on our mother. Wherever
we walk, we're walking on Mother Earth, so
wherever we are can be a holy sanctuary.

WHOLE BODY, WHOLE MIND

Don't pretend you're walking mindfully when in reality you're planning your grocery shopping or your next meeting. Walk with your whole body and mind. Each step contains insight. Each step has happiness. Each step has love— love and compassion for the Earth and for all beings, as well as for ourselves. Why do we walk like that? To be in touch with the great Earth, to be in touch with the world around us. When we're in touch, when we're fully aware of the wonder of walking on the Earth, each step nourishes and heals us. Thirty steps taken with this kind of insight are thirty opportunities to nourish and heal ourselves.

WAKING UP

Walking meditation is a way of waking up to the wonderful moment we are living in. If our minds are caught up and preoccupied with our worries and our suffering, or if we distract ourselves with other things while walking, we can't practice mindfulness; we can't enjoy the present moment. We're missing out on life. But if we're awake, then we'll see this is a wonderful moment that life has given us, the only moment in which life is available. We can value each step we take, and each step can bring us happiness because we're in touch with life, with the source of happiness, and with our beloved planet.

WALKING INSTEAD OF DRIVING

Sometimes we don't really need to use the car, but because we want to get away from ourselves, we go down and start the car. If we recite the phrase, "Before starting the car, I know where I am going," it can be like a flashlight—we may see that we don't need to go anywhere. You cannot escape yourself, wherever you go. Sometimes it's better to turn the engine off and go out for a walk. It may be more pleasant to do.

MASSAGING THE EARTH

When we walk mindfully, our feet are massaging the Earth. We sow seeds of joy and happiness with each step. With each step, a flower blooms.

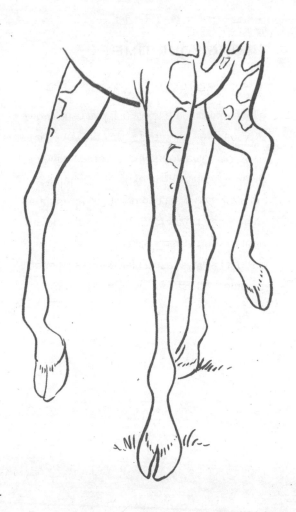

TAKING YOUR TIME

Allow enough time to walk. If you usually give yourself three minutes to get from your car to your door, give yourself eight or ten minutes. I always give myself an extra hour when I go to the airport so that I can practice walking meditation when I'm there. Sometimes my friends want to keep visiting right up to the last minute, but I always resist. I tell them that I need the time, and I say my good-byes early.

WALKING IS A CELEBRATION

When you walk, if you are aware that you are alive, that is already enlightenment. You are aware that you have a body; that is already enlightenment. You are aware that your feet are strong enough for you to enjoy walking; that is also enlightenment. When you walk, it can be a celebration. When you breathe like that, you are celebrating life.

WALKING WITH CHILDREN

Walking with children is a wonderful way to practice mindfulness. From time to time, a child may want to run ahead and then wait for you to catch up. A child is a bell of mindfulness, reminding us how marvelous life is. We can remind children that walking meditation is a wonderful way for them to calm down when they have strong feelings or are upset. We can walk with them without saying anything, just walking alongside. Our own breath is a gentle reminder for them to breathe with each step.

WALKING
MEDITATIONS

BREATHING AND WALKING

Our in-breath tends to be a little bit shorter than our out-breath. When you breathe in, take two or three steps. This is determined by your lungs. If your lungs want two steps as you breathe in, then give exactly two steps. If you feel better with three steps, then give yourself three steps. When you breathe out, you also listen to your lungs and let them determine how many steps you make while breathing out. In the beginning, practice two steps for the in-breath and three for the out-breath: *two, three; two, three; two, three*. Later on it may be *three, four* or *three, five*. If you feel you need to make one more step while breathing in, then allow yourself to enjoy one more step. When you feel that you want to make one more step

while breathing out, then allow yourself to add
another step as you breathe out. Every step
should be enjoyable.

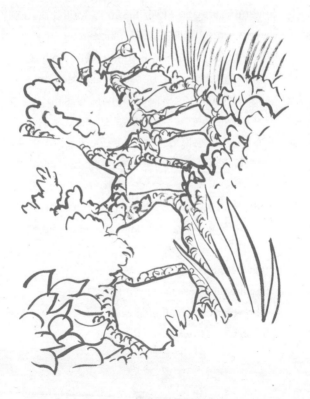

LETTING THE BUDDHA WALK

Several years ago, I was in Seoul, South Korea, to lead a large walking meditation in the city. When the time came to lead the walk, I found it very difficult to walk because hundreds of cameramen were closing in. There was no path to walk at all. I said, "Dear Buddha, I give up. You walk for me." The Buddha came right away and he walked. The path became clear. After this experience, I wrote a series of poems that can be used any time, but especially when walking or breathing is challenging.

Let the Buddha breathe,
Let the Buddha walk.
I don't have to breathe,
I don't have to walk.

The Buddha is breathing,
The Buddha is walking.
I enjoy the breathing,
I enjoy the walking.

Buddha is the breathing,
Buddha is the walking.
I am the breathing,
I am the walking.

There is only the breathing,
There is only the walking.
There is no one breathing,
There is no one walking.

Peace while breathing,
Peace while walking.
Peace is the breathing,
Peace is the walking.

WALKING WITH POEMS

You can walk using *gathas*, short practice poems. Combine your breath and your steps, and walk according to the rhythm of the poem. Arrange it so that the poems go rhythmically with your steps. Sometimes my in-breath is two steps and my out-breath is three steps. Sometimes my in-breath is three steps and my out-breath is four steps. Especially at the beginning, breathing out is always longer than breathing in. You can change the poem, adding or taking away words to match the rhythm of your steps. When you do jogging or running meditation, you can breathe in and make four steps, breathe out and make five steps. Dwell peacefully on the meaning of that poem in the present moment. Don't let your mind go far away. Don't try to be so poetic that you forget the practice. The main point of the practice is to cultivate more concentration.

In. Out.
Deep. Slow.
Calm. Ease.
Smile. Release.
Present moment.
Wonderful moment.

THE ISLAND OF SELF

The gatha I often take refuge in is, "Coming back to the island of myself." When life seems like a turbulent ocean, we have to remember we have an island of peace inside. Life has ups and downs, coming and going, gain and loss. Dwelling in the island of self, you are safe. When the Buddha was dying, he taught us not to take refuge in anything or anyone else, but to only take refuge in our own island. Breathing in, make two steps and say, "Taking refuge." Breathing out, make three steps and say, "In the island of self." Or change it to, "I go back. Taking refuge." You can always adjust whatever poem you've chosen to practice with.

Breathing in, I go back

to the island within myself.

There are beautiful trees

within the island.

There are clear streams of water.

There are birds,

sunshine and fresh air.

Breathing out, I feel safe.

I enjoy going back

to my island.

SLOW WALKING

When you are alone, you can practice slow walking meditation. Choose a distance of about three meters, or ten feet, and as you traverse that distance, take one step for each in-breath and one step for each out-breath. With the first step you can say silently, "I have arrived." With the next step, you can say silently, "I am home." If you aren't arriving one hundred percent in the here and now, stay there and don't make another step. Challenge yourself. Breathe in and out again until you feel you have arrived one hundred percent in the here and the now. Then smile a smile of victory. Then make a second step. This is to learn a new habit, the habit of living in the present moment.

FAMILY PRACTICE

Go out for a slow walk with your children before going to sleep. Just ten minutes is enough. If your children want to, you can hold hands as you walk. Your child will receive your concentration and stability, and you will receive his or her innocence and freshness. Young people might like to practice this simple poem while they walk. They can say to themselves, "Yes, yes, yes," as they breathe in, and, "Thanks, thanks, thanks," when they breathe out. I know many children who like this poem very much.

ARRIVING IN THE PRESENT MOMENT

Some of us don't need to use words to help us concentrate, but in the beginning of the practice it can be very helpful to make use of words. They help us to be concentrated, to be in the here and the now. When you take one in-breath, make two steps, and say to yourself: "I have arrived. I have arrived." Take one out-breath and make three steps, and say to yourself: "I am home. I am home. I am home." This is not a statement; this is a practice. Arrive in the here and the now, and make a strong determination to stop and not to run anymore. You can say, "Arrived, arrived," as you breathe in, and, "Home, home, home," as you breathe out. After spending some time with "Arrived, home," you can change to, "Here, now," and then to, "Solid, free."

I have arrived.

I am home

in the here,

in the now.

I am solid.

I am free.

In the ultimate

I dwell.

THE BEAUTIFUL PATH

The mind can go in a thousand directions.
But on this beautiful path, I walk in peace.
With each step, a gentle wind blows.
With each step, a flower blooms.

The mind darts from one thing to another, like a monkey swinging from branch to branch without stopping to rest. Thoughts have millions of pathways, and we are forever pulled along by them into the world of forgetfulness. If we can transform our walking path into a field for meditation, our feet will take every step in full awareness, our breathing will be in harmony with our steps, and our minds will naturally be at ease. Every step we take will reinforce our peace and joy and cause a stream of calm energy to flow through us.

TAKING REFUGE IN THE EARTH

When we can come back to ourselves and take refuge in our inner island, we become a home for ourselves and we become a refuge for others at the same time. Walking with one hundred percent of your body and mind can free you from anger, fear, and despair. Each step can express your love for the Earth. While walking, you can say,

> With each step,
> I come home to the Earth.
> With each step,
> I return to my source.
> With each step,
> I take refuge in Mother Earth.

Or, as you walk, you can say,

I love the Earth.
I am in love with the Earth.

A LETTER TO THE EARTH

Dear Mother Earth,

Every time I step upon the Earth, I will train myself to see that I am walking on you. Every time I place my feet on the Earth, I have a chance to be in touch with you and with all your wonders. With every step I can touch the fact that you aren't just beneath me, dear Mother, but you are also within me. Each mindful and gentle step can nourish me, heal me, and bring me into contact with myself and with you in the present moment.

Walking in this spirit, I can experience awakening. I can awaken to the fact that I am alive, and that life is a precious miracle. I can awaken to the fact that I am never alone and can never die. You are always there within me and around me at every step, nourishing me, embracing me, and carrying me far into the future. Dear Mother, I make the promise today to return your love and fulfill this wish by investing every step I take on you with love and tenderness. I am walking not merely on matter, but on spirit.

RELATED TITLES

Monastics and visitors practice the art of mindful living in the tradition of Thich Nhat Hanh at our ten mindfulness practice centers around the world. For a full listing of practice centers, or for information about retreats, visit plumvillage.org or contact:

Plum Village
33580 Dieulivol, France
plumvillage.org

Deer Park Monastery
Escondido, CA 92026, USA
deerparkmonastery.org

Magnolia Grove Monastery
Batesville, MS 38606, USA
magnoliagrovemonastery.org

Blue Cliff Monastery
Pine Bush, NY 12566, USA
bluecliffmonastery.org

European Institute of
Applied Buddhism
D-51545 Waldbröl, Germany
eiab.eu

Thailand Plum Village
Nakhon Ratchasima,
30130 Thailand
phfhk.org

The Mindfulness Bell, a journal of the art of mindful living in the tradition of Thich Nhat Hanh, is published three times a year by our community. To subscribe or to see the worldwide directory of Sanghas, or local mindfulness groups, visit mindfulnessbell.org.

The Thich Nhat Hanh Foundation supports Thich Nhat Hanh's peace work and mindfulness teachings around the world. For more information on how you can help or on how to nourish your mindfulness practice, visit the foundation at tnhf.org.

PARALLAX
PRESS

Parallax Press, a nonprofit publisher founded by
Zen Master Thich Nhat Hanh, publishes books
and media on the art of mindful living and
Engaged Buddhism. We are committed to offering
teachings that help transform suffering and
injustice. Our aspiration is to contribute to collective
insight and awakening, bringing about a more
joyful, healthy, and compassionate society.

View our entire library at **parallax.org**.